A colour guide to familiar

SEA AND COASTAL BIRDS

A colour guide to familiar
SEA AND COASTAL
BIRDS

By Jiří Felix

Illustrated by Květoslav Hísek

Translated by Olga Kuthanová
Graphic design: Soňa Valoušková

English version first published 1975 by
OCTOPUS BOOKS LIMITED
59 Grosvenor Street, London W1

ISBN 0 7064 0513 7

Printed in Czechoslovakia
3/10/14/51

CONTENTS

FOREWORD

This book acquaints the reader with sixty-four species of birds inhabiting the open seas, sea islands, seacoasts and in part also bodies of freshwater near the sea. The selection of the birds shown in this book was determined first and foremost by their occurrence at sea or on the seacoasts and was by no means simple or straightforward. Besides birds that spend their entire life on or near the sea we have included also certain species that breed in the northern tundras but otherwise are found at sea as well as certain typical birds of inland waters and swamps that migrate along the seacoasts or over the sea.

In the first part of this book the reader will learn about the body structure of sea birds, their biology, unusual aspects of their migration, as well as about 'bird cliffs', 'bird islands', and the like.

The pictorial section depicts the individual species — either the male in his nuptial plumage or both the male and female in cases of marked sexual dimorphism, the characteristic egg, and in some species also the nest. The text on the facing page acquaints the reader with the biological characteristics and habits of the bird, the nest structure, etc. The brief marginal note accompanying each colour plate offers a transcription of the individual bird's voice or song, size of the egg, the average length of its body measured from the tip of the bill to the tip of the tail, and in some instances also the wingspan, plus the flight silhouette.

WHAT ARE SEA AND COASTAL BIRDS?

Of the approximately 8,600 species of birds distributed throughout the world 285 are sea birds. The individual species are found either in the northern or southern hemisphere or else they are cosmopolitan. Typical inhabitants of the southern seas, for example, are the albatrosses and penguins, whereas alcids breed in the north, and the Caspian tern has a cosmopolitan distribution.

Marine birds are generally closely tied to the sea, spending practically their entire lives there and congregating to nest at regular places where food is abundant. Some species are very numerous, certain gulls and terns numbering as much as a million individuals, whereas others are very rare with a world population of less than one thousand, e.g. Audouin's gull *(Larus audouinii)* of the Mediterranean.

Coastal birds are found mostly on the seashore, during migration and in winter also on the edges of rivers, ponds and lakes. At this time they may be encountered even in central Europe, which they cross on their flight from the north to their southern wintering grounds. Chief of these are the waders, which have a world-wide distribution. Many breed on the seacoast as well as inland near freshwater.

Flamingos, which are found in shallows near the seashore as well as inland lakes, may also be considered as coastal birds. They occur in lowlands as well as high in the mountains even at altitudes of more than four thousand metres.

Other birds that may be classed in this group are certain raptors that hunt their prey largely near the coast and also nest there, e.g. the gyrfalcon.

Some birds found in bays or else on or near the seashore during the winter months, however, often nest far from the coast, for instance certain species of geese, ducks and swans. Others again, e.g. the white pelican, some members of the heron family and certain cormorants, breed in large river deltas. The snowy owl nests in the tundras, whence it occasionally travels, often in large numbers, to the coast after the nesting season. Some species of waders that breed in the northern tundras often converge in large numbers on the seashore during migration. All these birds, which are not exclusively marine species, may be encountered on the seashore at various times of the year.

HOW THE MORPHOLOGY OF SEA BIRDS IS ADAPTED TO LIFE ON THE WATER

The typical coloration, size and shape of the bill and tail, as well as the wings and feet make it possible not only to identify the various species of birds but also to determine their way of life. One can identify good fliers by the shape of the wings, good swimmers by the position of the legs at the rear, the webbed toes and their noticeable body immersion, and birds of prey by the beak and talons.

The body of sea birds is covered with feathers which in most species grow in definite tracts called pterylae. The intervening spaces, called apteria, are not evident at first glance because they are concealed by the contour feathers. The contour feathers, as the name implies, give the body its typical shape and include the flight feathers, tail feathers, etc. Underneath the contour feathers, there is a layer of fine down feathers. The feathers of sea birds are usually close-packed and grow thickly over the body thus serving as good heat insulation. Furthermore in most birds the feathers are lubricated by the secretion of the oil (uropygial) gland at the base of the tail. Birds spread this oil over their feathers by preening them with the bill. Sea birds and waterfowl do so regularly several times a day thus making the feathers impervious to water and keeping them from becoming soaked. Besides this the birds also bathe regularly to keep the feathers and skin from drying out. Those young birds that lack a functional uropygial gland waterproof their fine down by climbing through the feathers of the adult birds which are more strongly lubricated at this time and because preening is instinctive behaviour, they use their bills to spread over the entire body the oil which has rubbed off onto their feathers.

The feathers of all birds are replaced periodically and this process is called moulting. Old, worn feathers are shed as the new ones grow in. In many species the tail and flight feathers are shed successively so that the bird does not lose the power of flight. However, some birds such as divers, geese, ducks, swans and flamingos shed all their feathers at once and are incapable of flight for a period of three to seven weeks. Because they are easy prey for raptors at this time they conceal themselves in vegetation until the new flight feathers grow in.

Characteristics reflecting their attachment to water are not equally pronounced in all sea birds. Generally this is evident in the adaptation of the bird's anatomical structure to life on water. For example, in some species that are strongly tied to water, the feet have been transformed into excellent paddles and have almost completely lost the power of supporting the body. The wings of some serve not only for flight but also for swimming underwater with the tail acting as a rudder, being adapted accordingly. Anatomical adaptation to life in water, however, is not always evident at first glance, e. g. folds of skin in the nostrils preventing the entry of water during diving, and so on. The same holds true of a bird's physiological adaptation to its aquatic environment, which is of equal importance in the life of water birds.

The penguins, which inhabit the southern hemisphere, provide an interesting example of anatomical and physiological adaptation to an aquatic existence. They have lost the power of flight, the wings being used only as paddles, but they are superb swimmers. They swim with only their heads and the top of their backs visible and are thus able to submerge with lightning rapidity. Underwater they travel at amazing speeds of up to forty kilometres an hour and can capture even fast-swimming fish. They can leap up onto an ice floe or an elevated spot on the shore in an upright position after a rapid spurt underwater. Sometimes they leap out of the water in an arc, travelling in the manner of porpoises. Penguins with straight, strong, compressed bills feed mainly on fish, which they swallow whole. Others have long beaks with slightly downcurved tips and without sharp edges, e.g. the king penguin (Aptenodytes patagonica). These hunt mostly small crustaceans and molluscs at sea, though they also eat fish.

Divers, too, are superbly equipped for life in water, where

they spend practically all their time, coming ashore only to nest. They are very clumsy on land, practically crawling along on their bellies, for the legs are placed far to the rear, but this is compensated for by their rapid and skilled movement in water. They are not only good swimmers but excellent at diving as well. They have a streamlined torpedo-shaped body

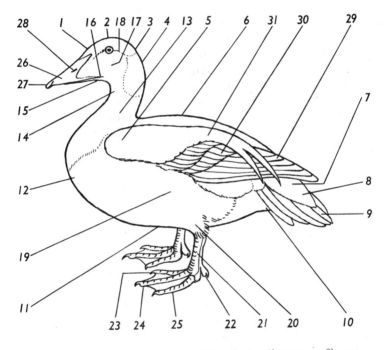

Fig. 1. Topography of the eider: 1) forehead, 2) crown, 3) nape, 4) hind neck, 5) shoulders, 6) back, 7) rump, 8) upper tail coverts, 9) tail quills, 10) under tail coverts, 11) belly, 12) breast, 13) neck, 14) throat, 15) chin, 16) lores, 17) cheek, 18) ear region, 19) flank, 20) shank, 21) tarsus, 22) hind toe, 23) inner toe, 24) middle toe, 25) outer toe, 26) bill, 27) nail, 28) nostrils. 29) primaries, 30) secondaries, 31) shoulder coverts.

well adapted to movement in water, and strong, webbed feet (the three front toes are joined), which they use as paddles. Though the wings are comparatively short and narrow, divers are swift, powerful and unswerving fliers. They take to the air from water, as they cannot rise from land and if it should happen that they alight on land during migration they are completely helpless. They fly with neck outstretched and the feet trailing behind the short tail. When swimming they insert their wings at the sides of the body in special pockets formed by elongated feathers. While moulting all the flight feathers are shed at once so that the birds go through a flightless period of several weeks. The beak is long, straight and pointed, and used to good advantage as a weapon of defence, often causing sharp wounds.

Typical inhabitants of the open seas are the Tubinares or tube-noses, which come to land only to nest, spending the greater part of their lives above or on the sea. They are superb fliers with long, narrow wings, capable of gliding for hours over the sea. Some of the smaller species fly close to the water without touching the surface. The feathers are closely packed and well oiled. The three front toes are united by a broad web. The bill is comparatively strong, with slightly downcurved tip, and nostrils extending in short tubes on top of the upper bill. The largest species, the wandering albatross, has the largest wingspan in the bird kingdom — 370 centimetres. Albatrosses are past masters at gliding flight, taking advantage of the air currents to travel swiftly and effortlessly without a single wingbeat. They also travel long distances of up to several thousand kilometres.

Also belonging to the group of tube-noses are the shearwaters and petrels, both excellent fliers and swimmers. The smallest of them all, the storm petrel, is only thirteen centimetres long, whereas the largest, the giant petrel, has a wingspan of about two metres. Many shearwaters skim for hours over the sea barely above the water. They also make lengthy migrations, leaving their breeding grounds and crossing the equator to the opposite hemisphere.

The birds of the group known as totipalmate swimmers (all

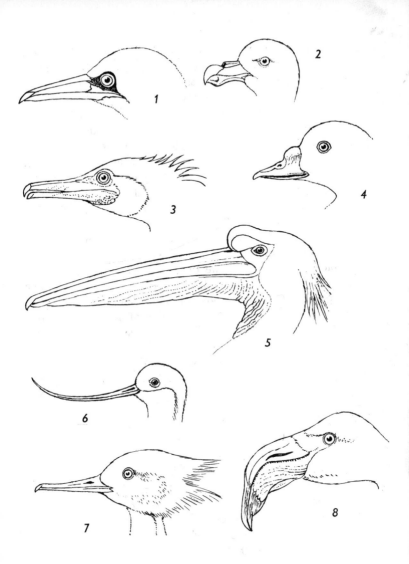

Fig. 2. Types of bills: 1. gannet, 2. fulmar, 3. cormorant, 4. common scoter, 5. white pelican, 6. avocet, 7. red-breasted merganser, 8. greater flamingo.

four toes united by a web) are also superbly adapted to aquatic life. They are divided into several families, each equipped by nature for a different method of obtaining aquatic food. This is naturally reflected in the general structure of the body as well as the individual parts.

Most striking of all, chiefly because of their peculiarly-shaped bills, are the pelicans. The bill is very long and slightly downcurved, the lower mandible consisting of two struts joined at the tip from which hangs a large, distensible pouch. Pelicans fly and swim with the head drawn back and the bill resting on the neck. The legs are comparatively short but strong.

Exclusively marine birds are the gannets. They have a streamlined body, short neck and fairly long, cone-shaped bill, which is a perfect tool for grasping the fish they catch. The wings are long and narrow and, as one would expect, gannets are expert fliers, spending hours above the water and often attaining speeds of eighty kilometres per hour. They are also excellent divers, descending to depths of about thirty metres.

The family of cormorants is found all over the world on seashores as well as on inland lakes, large ponds and rivers. These birds have a long neck and long, thin, sharply hooked bill, with which they catch the fish, their main diet. They also have a throat pouch. The short legs are located at the rear of the body and that is why they sit so upright on rocks and trees. The feathers are not well lubricated and get soaked rather easily. For this reason cormorants perch in an elevated spot with wings spread out to dry after they have finished hunting. Closely allied to the cormorants are the anhingas. However, their bills are longer, thinner and sharply pointed instead of hooked, the necks are longer and snake-like and the tail feathers are longer too. They swim very low in the water, often with only the head and neck above the surface. They are excellent divers.

Frigate-birds are among the best fliers of the tropical seas, as is evidenced by their long, narrow wings. They have imperfect oil glands that do not provide for proper lubrication of

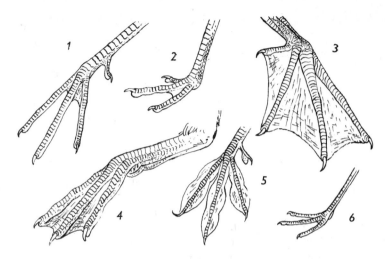

Fig. 3. Types of feet: 1. spotted redshank, 2. oystercatcher, 3. cormorant, 4. guillemot, 5. red-necked phalarope, 6. kentish plover.

the feathers, which soon become waterlogged. For this reason they seldom enter the water, spending all their time soaring over the ocean. They do not alight on the ground but only on the branches of trees from which they can take off easily. The wingspan is as much as 250 centimetres, which, in proportion to the body, is the largest in the bird kingdom.

Typical sea birds are the alcids, which spend most of their life at sea. They have very dense compact feathers, the legs are placed far back on the body, and the feet are webbed. On land they walk upright. Though they float quite high in the water they are nevertheless good divers. Underwater they swim beneath the surface very rapidly, propelling themselves with their feet and half-spread wings, which are narrow and comparatively short. The flight is rapid and direct, with swift wingbeats, the birds travelling close above the surface at speeds of about sixty to seventy kilometres per hour. Some alcids have a strong, compressed bill, well adapted for catching fish. Particularly striking is the large, parrot-like bill of the puffins, which during the breeding season swells at the base and turns a brilliant red, blue and yellow. After the breeding season the bright coloration is replaced mainly by yellow. The young have a much smaller conical beak at first; only later does it acquire the characteristic, compressed shape.

The terns are superb fliers with long, narrow, pointed wings and forked tail (in the majority of species). The body is slender and graceful, the bill straight and pointed, the legs short, and the feet webbed.

Several families of waders are also birds of the seashore. Common features include long legs (remarkably long in some species), small or lobate webs, and a small or atrophied hind toe. The body is slender, the bill of varying length — straight in some species, downcurved or upcurved in others — the wings comparatively long and narrow. Some waders are rapid and strong fliers, travelling as much as a thousand kilometres without a stop. Waders are usually found near water, on the seacoast, but some species make their home far inland. Typical marine waders are the phalaropes, with individual lobate webs on each toe. These birds spend most of their time on the sea, feeding on the floating organisms they pick from the surface. The underside of the body is thickly covered with close-packed feathers which provide perfect insulation against the cold of the water.

THE COLORATION OF SEA BIRDS

In some species of birds the male differs markedly in colour from the female, a phenomenon known as sexual dimorphism. Among water birds this is pronounced in ducks, whereas in the case of geese, swans, gulls, divers and alcids the male and female are alike. This is true also of most waders, though some have differently coloured plumage during the breeding season, e.g. the ruff, which grows a collar or 'ruff' of long, bright feathers in early spring as well as tufts of elongated feathers on the head resembling horns. The 'ruff' varies widely in colour and no two males are exactly alike.

Sexual dimorphism in phalaropes is unusual in that the female is larger and more brightly coloured than the male. In this instance it is the male who incubates the eggs without any aid from his mate, and it is a general rule of nature that the bird that incubates is more soberly coloured so as to escape the notice of enemies.

Some birds have two differently coloured garbs a year, for they moult twice annually — the one being a complete and the other a partial moult. Ducks are a particularly good example. In late spring the males generally shed all their feathers — the small ones as well as the flight and tail feathers — after which they resemble their duller mates, except for more brightly coloured, newly grown flight feathers. They moult a second time in the autumn, but only partially, retaining the flight feathers and shedding only small contour feathers to don the brightly coloured garb they will wear until the following spring.

Many birds, e.g. divers, certain species of waders as well as gulls, have a different colouring in winter. In their winter (eclipse) plumage the black-headed gull, little gull and other species have the head coloured white whereas in spring it is chocolate brown or black. Plovers and sandpipers exchange their bright and rich colours for various shades of grey in winter.

In many species of birds the young are coloured differently from the adults, acquiring the mature plumage in their second, third, or sometimes as late as their fourth year, e.g. gulls, the sea eagle and the bearded vulture.

MIGRATION

Birds are divided into the following basic groups, depending on whether they remain in their breeding grounds throughout the year or leave for the winter:

Resident birds — that never leave the general area of their nesting grounds.

Dispersive birds — that range far afield (often hundreds of kilometres) in all directions from their nesting grounds after the breeding season.

Migratory birds — that leave their nesting grounds each year in the autumn, fly in a specific direction to warmer quarters for the winter and return again in the spring.

Sea and coastal birds are usually tied even during migration to the sea or to rivers, inland lakes or ponds, where they always stop for a brief period to feed. They are known to journey remarkable distances. Results of ringing have shown that the winter quarters of the common tern *(Sterna hirundo)* may be as far as ten thousand kilometres from its nesting grounds.

The sandwich tern *(Sterna sandvicensis)*, which breeds on the coasts of the British Isles and the North and Baltic seas, flies along the western coast of Europe as far as South Africa for the winter.

The record journeys, however, are those made by the arctic tern *(Sterna paradisaea)*, which flies a distance of 36,000 kilometres to its winter quarters and back every year.

The albatrosses are also indefatigable travellers. One wandering albatross *(Diomedea exulans)* was captured 5,650 kilometres from the spot where it had been ringed twenty-two days previously, which means that it must have flown 257 kilometres a day. Albatrosses are not the only birds to make such long journeys. The golden plover *(Pluvialis apricaria)*,

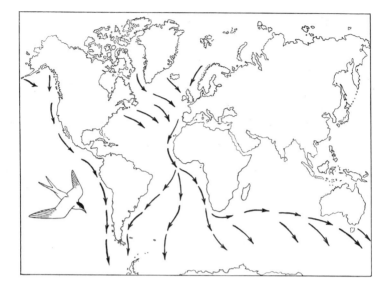

Fig. 4. Migration routes of the arctic tern

which breeds in northern Alaska on the shores of the Arctic Ocean, annually flies to Hawaii or the La Plata area in South America.

The lesser golden plover *(Pluvialis dominica),* which breeds in northern Siberia and North America, journeys all the way to southern Asia, to the Sunda Islands and thence as far as Australia; individuals breeding in arctic North America winter on the southernmost tip of South America. The turnstone *(Arenaria interpres)* of Scandinavia winters not only in southwestern Europe but also makes its way to the African coast southward as far as the Cape of Good Hope. The curlew *(Numenius arquata)* likewise flies as far as east and south Africa as does the ruff *(Philomachus pugnax).* Long journeys are also made by the red-necked phalarope *(Phalaropus lobatus),* its European populations wintering on the shores of the Aral Sea, eastern populations on the islands between southern Asia and Australia, and North American populations along the western coast of tropical South America. Likewise, the black-winged stilt *(Himantopus himantopus)* leaves its European nesting grounds for Africa and southern Asia in winter.

Flight is the general method of travel in the bird kingdom but some birds have lost the power of flight and if they are migratory are forced to travel by other means. Penguins, for instance, swim to their distant nesting grounds in the Antarctic every year. Some birds, even though able to fly, e. g. the gannet *(Sula bassana),* swim part of the way to their wintering grounds and fly the remainder. Their young, though unable to fly until they are 95 to 107 days old, abandon the nest at the age of about 75 days, leaping into the sea and swimming in the direction of migration. The eider *(Somateria mollissima),* as well as some divers, also swims to its southerly wintering grounds, as does also Brünnich's guillemot *(Uria lomvia),* which sometimes journeys hundreds of kilometres in this manner.

Only very occasionally are birds known to migrate in part by walking. In one instance thousands of American coots *(Fulica americana)* were observed walking for three days in the direction of their winter quarters. Other species of birds sometimes walk shorter distances.

Birds migrate mostly by night, and not only nocturnal birds but many diurnal species as well. Those that migrate chiefly in the hours of darkness are insectivorous birds and in great part ducks, geese and waders. Swallows, swifts, bee-eaters, storks and many diurnal raptors migrate in the daytime. Marine birds that fly across the vast expanses of the sea travel both by day and night.

The routes followed by birds crossing the Mediterranean generally lead via the straits or across islands directly southward. In deserts and steppes the routes lead through oases, which are regular stopping places on the way.

BREEDING AND NESTING

Courtship

Courtship usually begins after the birds' arrival at their nesting grounds, but in some species it begins in their winter quarters or during the return flight. Each species or given group of birds has a characteristic manner of courtship, which in many sea birds is very striking. The male cormorant sits on the partly built or completed nest, points his beak and tail upwards and jerks his wings in regular rhythm. As soon as the female approaches he throws his head on his back and utters a hollow groan. The female then comes closer with inflated throat pouch and head feathers erect, continuously uttering croaking sounds. Following copulation each lays its neck on its partner's.

Another striking example is the courtship performance of albatrosses, where the male and female stand facing each other, holding their heads erect and clapping their bills. Such 'greeting' of the partners is known in many other birds, e.g. the white stork. The albatrosses then touch or clash beaks, walk about each other with a rolling gait, flap their wings and

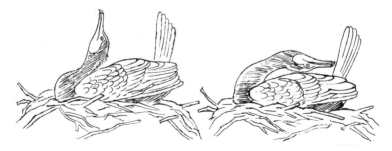

Fig. 5. Characteristic phases of the cormorant's courtship display.

point their beaks upwards. After this they spread their wings and shift their weight from one foot to the other in a sort of dance, with necks erect and beaks pointing upwards. They may continue these courtship antics even during incubation.

The courtship of ducks, too, is worth noting. In some species the male and female swim around each other, dive, nod their heads, immerse their bills in the water, jerk themselves erect, flutter their wings and lay their necks on the water. The performances are many and varied. At one stage of the goldeneye's courtship the drake throws his head on his back with his bill pointing upward, twitches it several times and often kicks up a spray of water with his feet. The courtship performance of the eider *(Somateria mollissima)* is also noteworthy. It usually takes place in the daytime, but often also on clear nights. The drake jerks his head up and down, then suddenly throws it on his back with his bill pointing upward at an angle, and after a while rights it again, all the while uttering sounds such as 'ahu' or 'uo'. Then he bows his head slightly, sounds his note, straightens his neck and stays motionless for a while in this position. After some time he lowers the bill almost to the water's surface and utters sounds resembling 'wu-huu'. Often he sprays water in front of him with his bill, bathes, sprays water on his back, preens the feathers on his back and sides and beats his wings against the water. Sometimes he also submerges for a brief moment. At other times he raises the front part of his body above the surface, spreads his wings wide and flaps them up and down. In group performances the males stage 'fights', flap their wings against the water and stretch their necks. Often they adopt threatening postures. During courtship the duck stretches her neck out over the water (the females of other species do this too — e.g. the goldeneye and mergansers). Then she also jerks her head up and down and occasionally sprays a few drops of water in front of her with the bill. The two birds then swim around each other in small circles.

Swans, on the other hand, swim towards each other and when they are close submerge their necks in the water a number of times and then entwine them.

Ruffs stage mock 'fights' amongst themselves, the males charging and fending with their ornamental feather 'ruffs' erected.

The Nesting Territory

Prior to nesting each pair of birds claims a certain nesting ground or territory which it defends against intruders, mostly birds of its own kind. In some species, however, e.g. certain geese, the males chase away any and every bird. Territorial boundaries are generally respected by other birds. If some bird trespasses into it then it is fiercely attacked by the established owner, who generally succeeds in ousting the intruder. The size of the nesting territory is not always the same. If food is abundant then the territories are smaller, if food is scarce they are larger. Some birds, chiefly sea and coastal species, however, nest in colonies that are often quite large. Here the nesting territory is limited to the nest itself or to its immediate vicinity. Many sea birds, such as the gannet *(Sula bassana)*, nest on narrow rock ledges where the nests are so tightly packed that there is often not enough room for all comers and numerous pairs either have to look elsewhere or do not nest at all. Most gulls and terns also form large colonies with the nests placed close to one another. Cormorants, auks, pelicans, guillemots, puffins and flamingos nest in colonies that number up to thousands of pairs. Birds that nest in colonies are not in competition with each other for food on or near the nesting site for they fly great distances, often several tens of kilometres, in search of food. Some species, such as cormorants and pelicans, even forage for food jointly, in groups. Flamingos fly far afield from their nesting site in their quest for food, and as for penguins, when incubating, one partner sits on the single egg and fasts for a number of days while the other swims far out to sea to feed.

Some species of sea birds nest in mixed colonies of two or more species of birds. Thus, for example, some terns form colonies within or close by a colony of gulls, feeling safer in the company of their stronger and more wary relatives. Guillemots, the razorbill and other sea birds likewise often nest in mixed colonies, and certain ducks and waders are fond of locating their nests near a colony of gulls or terns.

The Nest

Most birds construct nests in which they lay their eggs. The ability to construct a nest of a certain type is instinctive to the given species and birds need not be taught how to go about it. In some it is merely a shallow depression in the ground, whereas in others, chiefly the songbirds, it is a very complex structure. Sea and coastal birds usually build a simple nest. Brünnich's guillemot lays its single egg on bare rock, only sometimes placing a small stone, twig or grass stem underneath. The eggs of Brünnich's guillemot and the razorbill are

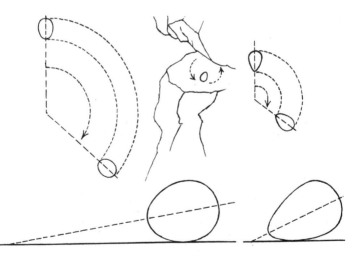

Fig. 6. Pear-shaped alcid's egg rotates in a much smaller circle than eggs of most other birds.

pear-shaped so that they rotate in a small circle around the pointed end and cannot roll off the rock ledge. Besides that the shell is very thick at the pointed end which gives the egg greater stability. Terns that nest on the seashore, e.g. the sandwich tern, often lay their eggs in a shallow depression lined only sparingly or not at all. Gulls build more solid nests, notably the kittiwake, which, unlike other species, nests on extremely narrow rock ledges. Appropriately its nest is plastered together with mud and thus very sturdy. The nests of gulls that breed on islands are lined very sparingly, whereas those that are located in shallows are tall structures of reeds. Very occasionally gulls will build their nests in trees, e.g. Bonaparte's gull *(Larus philadelphia)*. Huge structures are built in shallows by swans and in reeds by pelicans. Cormorants locate their nests either on coastal cliffs, where they are only sparingly lined as a rule, or in tall trees, where the structure of sticks and twigs is quite tall and large. Striking nests of mud, leaves, sand, and the like, are built in shallows by the flamingos; these are tall structures up to half a metre in height.

Some sea birds nest in various cavities. The goldeneye prefers rather large tree holes, often more than ten metres above the ground, generally these being cavities abandoned by the black woodpecker. As a rule the birds do not line the cavity but the female surrounds the eggs with down feathers. The goldeneye is also fond of nesting in man-made nest-boxes. The goosander, too, likes to nest in tree holes, but when these are scarce it will even make use of a rock cavity or even a hole in the ground. Likewise, several species of shearwater, e.g. Manx shearwater *(Puffinus puffinus)*, nest in ground burrows or rock crevices. Puffins nest in similar ground burrows or else in the burrows of mammals, also just between stones; in softer ground they sometimes even dig their own burrows.

Most ducks build their nest in grass tussocks, under a bush or between stones. The nest is well lined and the eggs are covered with down feathers that serve to insulate them against cold when the adult birds leave the nest for a time. Most geese build their nests in a similar manner. The common shelduck, however, nests in the abandoned burrows of mammals, and sometimes even in a small space between stones or under a fallen tree.

The sea eagle builds its nest either in trees, where it measures up to 1.5 metres in height and 2 metres across, or on a rock ledge, where it is much smaller.

The Eggs

The colouring, shape and usually also the number of eggs laid are characteristic for the given species in most cases. Some species, however, show a marked variation in the colouring of the eggs. For example the eggs of gulls, terns and above all alcids show such a great diversity of colour that only two out of a thousand have similar colouring. Other species of birds, on the other hand, have eggs of a single colour. In general it may be said that birds nesting in cavities or those that cover their nests on leaving them, e.g. ducks, do not need their eggs to have cryptic colours, unlike those species that lay their eggs in the open and leave them uncovered; the latter's eggs are thus spotted, streaked, speckled and the like, to merge with their surroundings and escape the notice of enemies. For example, the eggs of the Kentish plover are practically impossible to spot amongst the surrounding pebbles. The same is true of the eggs of the other species of waders. Owls, storks and pelicans have pure white eggs. These, however, lose their whiteness during incubation, sometimes acquiring even a dark brown hue, such as the eggs of the black-necked grebe, which become stained by the damp decaying vegetation in the nest. The eggs of cormorants and pelicans become coated with a chalky layer during incubation.

Some birds lay a specific number of eggs that is usually constant. The avocet, curlew and lapwing generally lay four eggs, the Kentish plover three. Sometimes, of course, there may be fewer eggs in the nest, for example if the first clutch is destroyed the second one may not contain the full number. At other times there may be more — when two females lay their eggs in the same nest. In the case of gulls the full clutch contains three eggs, terns lay two to three eggs, divers usually only two. Many sea birds lay only a single egg, e.g. the storm petrel, gannet and roseate flamingo. Ducks, on the other hand, lay a great number of eggs, usually about ten, but sometimes even more than twenty, for their young are preyed on by many enemies and therefore suffer great losses. In some species the number of eggs laid depends on the abundance of food. Thus, the snowy owl generally lays four to six eggs; when food is scarce, however, it lays only three or does not nest at all, whereas when lemmings, the owl's chief food, are plentiful the clutch contains as many as fifteen eggs.

In some species, e.g. ducks and geese, only the female incubates, whereas in others the partners take turns incubating, which is true of alcids, terns, gulls, pelicans and cormorants, and in rare instances, e.g. the red-necked phalarope and the dotterel, the eggs are incubated solely by the male. Some birds make no nest but carry their single egg with them all the time, e.g. the emperor penguin holds its egg in an abdominal pouch formed by a fold of the skin, supporting it from below by its feet.

The incubation period, i.e. the time when the birds sit on the eggs until they hatch, is comparatively long in the case of sea birds. Alcids incubate about thirty-five days, puffins thirty-seven days, the gannet forty days, shearwaters and petrels even more than sixty days, and the emperor penguin sixty-three days. The longest period of incubation, however, is that of the albatross — about eighty days.

The Young

Birds are divided into two separate groups according to the degree of development at hatching. The nestlings of the first group are hatched in a condition that enables them to leave the nest and follow their parents about almost as soon as they have dried. They feed themselves from the very first, being dependent on their parents only for protection from enemies, bad weather, and the like; the parents also guide them to spots where food is to be found. In the case of ducks and grebes the parents also provide the necessary lubrication for their offspring's feathers. This group of birds is called nidifugous.

The young of the second group, known as nidicolous birds, are entirely dependent on their parents, which bring them food for a certain period of time. In many species the young are hatched with practically no feathers and the parents must also keep them warm, e.g. pelicans and cormorants. In other species, as for instance in terns, gulls, alcids, birds of prey and owls, the young are hatched with a thick coat of down which keeps the cold out.

The young of many nidicolous birds remain in the nest for a certain period that is specific for each species but varies greatly amongst various species or groups of birds. In the case of the herring gull and common gull the young leave the nest after $1/2$ to $2^1/2$ days, scattering and sometimes concealing themselves in the neighbourhood; they may also swim. If undisturbed, however, they remain in the nest even longer. The young of the kittiwake, on the other hand, remain in the nest about thirty-five days, lying in one spot the whole time, later sometimes standing, but not daring to take a single step. The reason for this is that the nest is located on rock ledges on very steep cliffs where the flightless nestlings would meet certain death were they to fall. Another unusual feature distinguishing the young of the kittiwake is that their colouring is silvery and very conspicuous, for unlike the young of other gulls which are speckled and provided with protective colouring, they are less exposed to the danger of attack by any carnivore or bird of prey.

The young of many nidicolous sea birds remain in the nest quite a long time compared with other birds. For instance, skua nestlings remain in the nest for five to seven weeks, those of shearwaters more than two months, the young of the gannet seventy-five, and the young of albatrosses a full 240 days — the longest known period in the bird kingdom.

Birds nesting in colonies, as has already been said, often place their nests very close to one another. Sometimes there are as many as a thousand in a single colony and yet the birds unerringly locate their own nest. As a rule the size and colouring of the eggs is of no importance, as witness the example of gulls that attempted to move to the nest an artificial egg placed nearby which was several times the size of their own, or gulls that settled on their nests even when they contained other birds' eggs or pebbles. Most birds cannot recognize their own eggs but are familiar with the surroundings of the nest.

How, then, are birds able to identify their offspring? The young of most gulls, for example, scatter in the neighbourhood the day after hatching and are brought food by their parents. When a young nestling goes astray it is pecked, chased away and sometimes even killed by the other gulls but only if it is more than five days old. Before that gulls will feed not only their own but also other offspring. The adult birds recognize the particular voices of their young and can identify them amidst the many others that sound the same to the human ear. Hearing, as we see, plays an important role in the lives of most birds. Parent birds are able to distinguish the voice of their offspring which can be heard while they are still inside the shell.

Most nestlings do not learn to recognize their parents until several hours after they have hatched, at which time the image of the adult birds — their body shape, colouring and voice — becomes imprinted in their memory. Many nestlings will accept as parents birds of other species or even man. In the case of ducks the young drakes impress the likeness of the duck upon their memory not only as a mother but also as a female so that in the wild, when the time comes, they select a mate of their own kind and there is little danger of crossbreeding, which is quite common in captivity where the young of several non-related species are often kept in the same aviary.

HOW AND WHAT SEA BIRDS EAT

Most sea birds obtain their food at sea or on the seacoast. Many species feed solely on fish or else fish form a greater or lesser portion of their diet.

Alcids feed primarily on fish. Puffins hunt mostly small herrings, often carrying ten to twelve in their beaks at a time. People have long wondered how a puffin can hold so many fish without any slipping from its grasp as it takes up another. The explanation is simple — the fish's head is held fast between the tongue and edge of the bill thus enabling the bird to open its bill and catch further fish without any trouble. The puffin pursues its prey under water, propelling itself with both wings and feet at such speeds that few fish escape. It also eats various molluscs and crustaceans.

Gannets feed almost exclusively on fish. With their wings pressed close to the body they plummet in a steep dive from heights of twenty to thirty metres into the water in pursuit of their prey. Sometimes they dive to remarkable depths, sometimes as great as thirty metres.

Pelicans, too, feed mainly on fish, and are very well equipped for fishing in strength. When fishing, a flock of pelicans forms a semi-circle and advances towards the shore, the birds beating the water with their wings and stabbing at it now and then with their long bills. The fish are thus trapped in the shallows where the birds scoop them up with their beaks into their distensible pouches. Some species, such as the brown pelican *(Pelecanus occidentalis),* cruise in circles above the water seeking their prey. On sighting a fish near the surface they abruptly press their wings to the body and plunge downwards, often submerging completely for a few seconds.

Cormorants, too, are expert fishers, which like the gannets can dive to depths of as much as thirty metres in pursuit of their prey. Having caught it they swim to the surface before swallowing it. The cormorants' remarkable insatiable appetite was put to good use by fishermen in China and Japan. A common technique was to tie around the base of the bird's neck a thong attached to a long tether which the fisherman held in his hand. When the cormorant surfaced after diving for fish the thong was pulled tight to prevent it from swallowing the catch and the fisherman took the fish from its gullet. The usual method was to fish from a boat with a team of about twelve trained birds. In Japan cormorants have been used to fish in this manner on rivers since the sixth century. In medieval days fishing with cormorants was a popular sport even on the River Thames in Great Britain.

Anhingas catch fish in an interesting manner by impaling the prey underwater with a darting movement of their sharp-pointed beak and then bringing it to the surface.

Frigate-birds likewise hunt fish, snatching them from the sea surface or out of the air in the case of flying fish. Besides that, being expert fliers, they chase other birds such as gulls, terns, gannets and pelicans, harassing them until they drop their prey which the frigate-birds then scoop out of mid-air.

Skuas, too, chase gulls and terns to rob them of their catch. However, they also feed on small vertebrates and insects as well as on the eggs of other birds.

Large gulls eat mostly animal food and fish, often following in the wake of ocean-going liners or circling above fishing boats, waiting for refuse thrown overboard, especially remnants of fish. Some species of gulls often eat vegetable food as well.

The mainstay of the terns' diet is small fish, which the birds catch near the surface by plunge-diving into the water.

An interesting structural adaptation for fishing is exhibited by the bill of the skimmers (Rynchopidae), which is laterally compressed, with the lower mandible much longer than the upper one. The birds obtain their food by skimming close to the water with the lower mandible just cutting the surface to catch any of the various invertebrates and fish that cross their path.

The methods whereby some waders obtain their food are

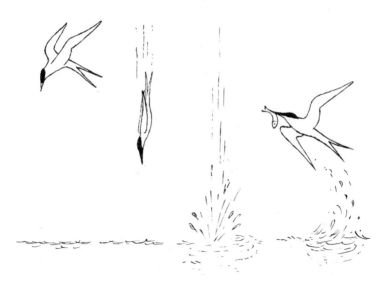

Fig. 7. Tern plummeting after a fish.

quite striking. The avocet wades in the shallows, stamping its feet on the sandy or muddy bottom and stirring up countless aquatic invertebrate animals, mainly various small crustaceans, which it collects with rapid sweeping movements of its upcurved bill.

Also specially adapted is the powerful bill of the oystercatcher, which is long and vertically flattened, and used for probing in the mud and sand of the shore for worms and molluscs as well as for opening mussels and clams or chiselling limpets off rocks. Whole flocks of oystercatchers may be seen running about on the shore at ebb tide wherever there is an abundance of marine molluscs.

The eider is well equipped for obtaining food underwater with a fairly short but deep, powerful bill. It hunts at depths of as much as ten metres, mostly various molluscs and crustaceans. It can break off and crush even mussels, cockles and other thick-shelled bivalves as well as the armour of crustaceans.

Mergansers are also underwater hunters and have a long, narrow bill with serrations on the edges — an excellent tool for catching fish and other aquatic animals.

BIRD CLIFFS AND BIRD ISLANDS

Over millions of years, the surf pounding on the seacoasts has carved out bizarre rock formations and steep cliffs. Such generally inaccessible places have become a refuge for sea birds during their nesting period. Rocky islands and cliffs of this sort are also found on the western and northern coasts of Europe. These cliffs might be termed bird cliffs for they are literally covered with birds during the breeding season and individual pairs are often hard put to establish their tiny nesting territory. The nests are often crowded side by side and the air is filled with the shrill clamour of many birds.

Bird cliffs are to be found in practically all the seas, on islands as well as mainland coasts. Some small islands, such as Mafadrangur off the southern coast of Iceland or Sulnasker, Eldey and Noss in the Shetlands, are practically inaccessible for quadrupeds and man alike. Here, the birds are excellently protected against enemies, except of course from raptors, robber gulls and skuas that can get at them from the air, and as a result the bird populations sometimes attain vast numbers.

Let us take a look at several species that form the largest colonies: St. Kilda (in the Hebrides) is at present the site of the largest colony of gannets *(Sula bassana)* numbering about thirty thousand birds. The razorbill *(Alca torda)* is never very plentiful at any place but the largest colonies off the Norwegian coast on the cliffs in the Syltefjord number about ten thousand birds, the same number nesting on the island of Vedoy (Lofoten). Far more plentiful is Brünnich's guillemot *(Uria lomvia),* with an estimated population of some two million on the coasts of Greenland and the same in Novaya Zemlya. Its relative, the common guillemot *(Uria aalge)* is not as plentiful; 'only' a hundred thousand of these birds breed in the Syltefjord in arctic Norway. The puffin *(Fratercula arctica),* on the other hand, is quite a different proposition —

about two-and-a-half million birds breed in Iceland and the Faroes, some four million in the British Isles, and the entire world population numbers some fifteen million. Other bird cliff dwellers include the lovely tufted puffin *(Lunda cirrhata)*, which digs nesting burrows, the little auk *(Plautus alle)*, smallest of the alcids — weighing a mere 120 to 130 grams, the kittiwake *(Rissa tridactyla)*, which breeds only in colonies of its own kind, the great black-backed gull *(Larus marinus)* nesting on broader rock ledges, the shag *(Phalacrocorax aristotelis)* and the cormorant *(Phalacrocorax carbo)*, nesting in colonies often on sheer cliffs rising straight up from the sea. Other species of European sea birds are not as plentiful on bird cliffs.

Huge colonies of sea birds nesting on rocky islands and seacoasts are found not only in the northern but in the southern hemisphere as well. There, many sea birds are rigidly protected by law and some large colonies are even guarded by armed sentries. Fishing, moreover, is sometimes prohibited in areas where fish-eating birds forage for food. Such measures would doubtless be welcomed by conservationists everywhere. Here, however, the protective measures are not the work of dedicated conservationists but of powerful companies which the birds provide with an annual income of millions of dollars in the form of guano, the most precious of natural fertilizers. Guano is the accumulated, decomposed and dry excreta of birds that feed on fish. The most in demand was that harvested on the coasts of Peru, where the layers deposited on the off-shore islands by nesting birds over thousands of years were thirty to sixty metres thick. Access to the islands had already been strictly prohibited long ago by Inca rulers, thus ensuring a peaceful haven for the birds, which returned there every year to nest. The dry climate also kept the bird excreta from being washed away. And so when colonizers set foot on these islands in 1790 they discovered vast quantities of guano there. However, it was not till 1840 that the guano began to be harvested on a large scale, with five hundred thousand tons being shipped annually to Europe between the years 1860 and 1880. At this rate, and what with the disturbance of the birds on the islands during the nesting period, the rich stores of guano would soon have been a thing of the past and so the government of Peru proclaimed the islands a strict nature preserve and prohibited not only the harvesting of guano during the nesting period but also disturbance of the birds in any way. Nowadays guano is harvested only on uninhabited islands or in places where the birds have already departed for the open sea after raising their offspring. Even so, however, yields have dropped markedly, for the rich stores have been practically exhausted and it has become a far less profitable industry. The principal and most numerous inhabitant of these islands is the guanay cormorant *(Phalacrocorax bougainvillei)*, which nests only in dry locations on islets off the coast of Peru where rain falls only two days a year. The cold rich current flowing past these islands attracts great numbers of small fish thus providing the birds with a continual abundance of food. That is why so many fish-eating birds are to be found there during the breeding season. It was determined that a single colony on an island numbers as many as ten million birds, with as many as three nests per square metre. One colony consumes up to 2,500 tons of fish a day.

Extensive sandy and stony beaches and countless small islands scattered in all the oceans are visited by further thousands of sea birds during the nesting period. Known as bird islands, they are inhabited mainly by the sandwich tern *(Sterna sandvicensis)* and roseate tern *(Sterna dougallii)*, which spend their entire lives on the seacoast; also the arctic tern *(Sterna paradisaea)*, Caspian tern *(Hydroprogne caspia)* and certain species of gulls, e. g. the common gull *(Larus canus)* and herring gull *(Larus argentatus)*.

Other birds that nest in colonies on seashores and islands, but also individually, include the avocet *(Recurvirostra avosetta)* and the black-winged stilt *(Himantopus himantopus)*.

The inhabitants of bird islands and bird cliffs are among the most numerous species in the bird kingdom.

The plates depict 64 species of birds. In those cases where the coloration of the male differs from that of the female (sexual dimorphism) both are shown. Also included is a colour illustration of the typical egg of the given species and sometimes a pen-and-ink drawing of the nest. The plates are arranged according to the zoological system of classification. The text accompanying each plate gives the basic biological data about the given species as well as items of particular interest. The column at top right gives the average length of the bird in centimetres, measured from the tip of the bill to the tip of the tail, the bird's coloration, a verbal description of the song and dimensions of the egg. These dimensions are given in millimetres, e.g. 15.5 — 19.5 × 12.0 — 14.4 mm, the first figure denoting the minimum length of the egg, the second the maximum length, the third the minimum width and the fourth the maximum width.

Where two common names are given the second refers to the American where it differs from the English.

Black-throated Diver — Arctic Loon

Gavia arctica

Gaviidae

The black-throated diver inhabits northern Europe and northwestern Asia. It also breeds in Scotland and in rare instances also in Pomerania in northern Germany and Poland. During the breeding season it is found on lakes, generally near the seacoast. The nest is placed on islets near deep water. It is only a shallow depression in grass, usually without any lining, and is generally right by the water's edge so that the birds can slip straight into the water from the nest. The one to two, sometimes three eggs are laid in April or May. The partners take turns incubating for twenty-eight to thirty-two days. On hatching the chicks take to the water with their parents, who guide them around for two months. When the young are fully grown the divers form small groups. Birds from the extreme northern areas abandon their nesting grounds as early as mid-August, often while the young are still unable to fly, swimming with them down the rivers to the sea and on along the coast. The main migration to the wintering grounds is usually in November, the birds returning again to their breeding grounds between early March and late April. They pass the winter on the Baltic, North and Mediterranean Seas as well as in the northern parts of the Black and Caspian Seas. During the migratory season single individuals may be seen fairly regularly even inland on ice-free water. The black-throated diver feeds mainly on fish, but also crustaceans and molluscs and on occasion even frogs, worms and aquatic insects. It sometimes dives to depths of forty-five metres in pursuit of prey.

Length:
58 to 69 cm.
The male and female have like plumage. Inconspicuous winter plumage.
Voice:
A deep, barking 'kwow' and the like; in flight a goose-like 'ga-ga-ga'.
Size of Egg:
75.7 — 95.7 × 45.5 — 56.0 mm.

Red-throated Diver — Red-throated Loon
Gavia stellata

The red-throated diver is at home in Iceland, northern Scotland, Ireland, Scandinavia, the Hebrides, Orkneys and Shetlands as well as in the Murmansk region. It is also found in Greenland and in the arctic regions of North America. It nests on the edges of small but deep pools, coastal lagoons and lakes. The nest is made of sphagnum, other mosses and plant stems and is always placed near water, sometimes even right on the water. Paired birds often return to the same spot every year. In May or June the female usually lays two eggs which both partners take turns incubating for about twenty-eight, sometimes even thirty-six days. They start incubating as soon as the first egg is laid. If the clutch is lost the female lays new eggs. The red-throated diver is a migratory bird; in the southern parts of its range it is a dispersive bird. European populations winter on the Atlantic coast as far as southern Spain, as well as in the North and Baltic, Mediterranean and Black Seas. During the migrating season the red-throated diver occurs as a vagrant also on inland bodies of water, where, however, it usually remains only a few days. The mainstay of the diet is fish, mostly seafish such as herring, sprats and cod, though the birds feed also on amphibians, crustaceans, molluscs, aquatic insects and worms.

Length:
53 to 61 cm.
The male and female have like plumage.
Winter plumage sober.
Voice:
A repeated quacking 'kwuck', also a thin, high wailing.
Size of Egg:
65.0 — 86.0
× 41.0 — 51.0 mm.

Manx Shearwater

Puffinus puffinus

Procellariidae

The Manx shearwater is widespread in Iceland, the Faroes, Shetlands and Orkneys, the west coast of Britain and Ireland as well as in Brittany and on smaller islands in the Mediterranean. It is both a dispersive bird and a migrant. On its migratory flights it often occurs on the coasts of the North and Baltic Seas as well as on the Portuguese coast; single individuals sometimes occur as vagrants even inland. Outside the breeding season it spends its time on the open sea or near the shore. When it is time for nesting the birds arrive in flocks at their breeding grounds in February and March, settling in large colonies on cliffs and rocky islands whence they fly out to sea. The Manx shearwater nests in burrows in the ground or in rock crevices. Often it digs these burrows itself, sometimes even in very hard ground, with both partners doing their bit; the actual nesting hollow is lined with feathers, leaves and grass. The single, white egg is laid in April or May, sometimes, though rarely, even in early June. The partners take turns incubating for stretches of three to five days as a rule, the bird on the nest going without food or water throughout its shift, while the other flies in search of food sometimes for distances of more than a thousand kilometres. The young hatch after fifty-one to sixty-one days and leave the nest at the age of ten weeks, though they are only able to leap into the water, being as yet incapable of flight. The flight feathers grow in later. The diet of the Manx shearwater consists of small fish, crustaceans and molluscs.

Length:
36 cm.
The male and female have like plumage.
Voice:
Various crooning and crowing notes.
Size of Egg:
54.5 — 65.7
× 39.2 — 45.1 mm.

Fulmar

Fulmarus glacialis

Iceland, Ireland, Great Britain, Brittany, the western coast of Norway, Greenland and Novaya Zemlya in the Arctic Ocean are the home of the stocky fulmar, which, however, is found here only during the breeding season, for otherwise it keeps to the open seas. It is both a dispersive as well as a migratory bird, arriving at its nesting grounds any time from December to April but keeping to the shore. It is not until the end of April (more often in May or early June) that it builds its nest on rocky sea islands or coastal cliffs. It nests in colonies sometimes numbering hundreds and even thousands of birds with nests spaced one to five metres apart. The actual nest is unlined and placed on a rocky ledge. The female lays one egg (occasionally two), which the partners take turns incubating for about fifty-two days. The young are fed only once a day and during the first two weeks are kept warm by one or the other of the parents. They leave the nest after forty-eight to fifty-seven days already capable of flight, but do not attain maturity until the age of seven years. The fulmar feeds on pelagic molluscs, crustaceans, also fish etc., which it generally gathers from the water's surface. It dives only rarely and then to a depth of one metre at the most.

Length:
47 cm.
The male and female have like plumage.
Voice:
A hoarse chuckling as 'ag-ag-ag-arrr'.
Size of Egg:
67.0 — 81.5
× 43.2 — 54.8 mm.

Storm Petrel

Hydrobates pelagicus

The eastern North Atlantic and western Mediterranean waters are where the storm petrel is found, which except in the breeding season inhabits the open seas. In winter it flies as far as the west and south coasts of Africa, but single individuals remain in the area of their breeding grounds throughout the year. On occasion it may occur as a vagrant as far inland as central Europe. It generally arrives at the small rocky islands where it breeds in late April but even before that it often occurs at sea in their vicinity. The storm petrel nests in ground burrows, rock crevices, rabbit holes, below rock ledges, etc. Only rarely does it dig its own hole. The female lays a single egg in late May or early June, though sometimes as late as the end of August. If the egg is lost a new one may be laid as late as September. Both partners take turns incubating. The young hatch after thirty-eight to forty-one days and are fed by the parents every night.

Storm petrels are most active between the hours of 10:30 p.m. and 3:30 a.m., even outside the breeding season. One of the parents remains in constant attendance upon the chick until it is thirty days old and then it is left by itself. The young bird abandons the nest after fifty-four to sixty-eight days. The diet consists of small cephalopods, crustaceans, molluscs, small fish and insects.

Its closest American relative is Leach's petrel *(Oceanodroma leucorhoa)*.

Length:
15 cm.
The male and female have like plumage.
Voice:
At the breeding grounds rasping, buzzing and grunting sounds such as 'hikav', 'ti-ti-tihk-ti-ti-tihk', 'arrr-r-r-r'.
Size of Egg:
25.0 — 30.7 × 19.0 — 23.0 mm.

Gannet or Solan Goose

Sula bassana

Sulidae

The gannet's European breeding grounds are located on the coast of Ireland, England, Scotland, Brittany, Norway, Iceland, and Faroe Islands and other small islands in this area. It is a sea bird that spends practically its whole life on the open sea. Young birds sometimes stray inland. The gannet arrives at its breeding grounds between February and early April. Large colonies of nesting birds may be seen in the British Isles, Iceland, and on rocky islands, usually in an open, elevated spot, from the end of March until May. The nest is made of seaweed, grass, bits of wood, etc. There may be as many as two to three nests to a square metre in such a colony. The female lays a single, thick-shelled egg, which both partners take turns incubating for thirty-nine to forty-six days. It sometimes takes more than a day for the chick to peck its way out and sometimes another three days before it opens its eyes. It is covered with a thin coat of down and is fed by the adult birds even at night. When feeding it thrusts its head into the throat of the parent bird. At the age of eleven weeks the chick is nice and plump and weighs one kilogram more than the adult bird. It abandons the nest at the age of seventy-five days, as yet incapable of flight but able to swim. Sometimes it swims as much as seventy kilometres from the nesting site before taking to the air, usually at the age of ninety-five to 107 days. On abandoning the colony the young gannet must fend for itself. It catches mainly herring, mackerel and sardines, both during the day and at night. It is an excellent diver.

Length:
91.5 cm.
Weight:
3 to 3.5 kg. The male and female have like plumage. The young bird is spotted.
Voice:
Usually a barking sound 'arrah' and similar noises.
Size of Egg:
62.0 — 87.5 × 41.0 — 54.0 mm.

Cormorant — Great Cormorant
Phalacrocorax carbo

Phalacrocoracidae

Asia, Europe and North America are where the cormorant breeds. In Europe it is found in large numbers on the seacoast but it also occurs inland on rivers and still bodies of water. It is both a dispersive and a migratory bird. When migrating it keeps close to the shoreline. It nests in colonies on rocky islands, often together with gannets, as well as in trees. Colonies may number as many as several thousand pairs of birds. Inland it is often found in heron colonies. Nests on rock ledges are only sparingly lined, nests in trees are woven of twigs and grass stems. Often the cormorant will build a new nest, but using the old foundation. Both partners take part in building the nest, and in tree colonies break off twigs with their strong beaks. The female usually lays three to five eggs between April and June, the two partners taking turns incubating them for twenty-three to twenty-nine days. The chicks do not open their eyes until three days after hatching. They take their food from the parents' throats. After thirty-five to fifty-six days in the nest they form flocks and range widely together with the adult birds. The cormorant feeds mostly on fish, occasionally also on crustaceans, and above all crabs, which it sometimes catches in great numbers. It hunts in small groups, frequently of about eight birds, which chase the fish towards one another. In parts of its range, it is often found in the company of pelicans, which do not dive, whereas cormorants pursue their prey underwater. Undigested bones and scales are regurgitated.

Length:
91.5 cm.
The male and female have like plumage.
Voice:
Various guttural groans like 'r-rah'.
Size of Egg:
56.2 — 70.8
× 33.8 — 44.4 mm.

Shag
Phalacrocorax aristotelis

The shag is widely distributed on the western coast of the Murmansk region, in Norway, Iceland, the British Isles, Ireland, the coast of western Europe as far as the islands of the Mediterranean and also on the coast of southeastern Europe. In some places it is resident, in others a dispersive bird. It is found exclusively on seacoasts, mainly ones with steep rocky cliffs. In winter it is also found on the coasts of the North and Baltic Seas. Only rarely does it stray inland. It nests in looser colonies than the common cormorant. The nest, made of seaweed, grass, leaves and small twigs, is placed on rock ledges. As a rule the female lays two to six eggs between the beginning of April and end of June, which the partners take turns incubating for thirty to thirty-two days. Within half an hour of hatching the young are already clamouring for food, which the parents give them three to four times daily. The young feed by thrusting their heads into the throats of the parent birds. They remain in the nest for forty-seven to fifty days and then take to the water, though they are as yet unable to fly. They begin to try their wings at the age of fifty-five to fifty-eight days. The rate of mortality among the young is high — as many as eighty per cent may die during the first year, whereas that of adult birds is around fourteen per cent. The shag feeds exclusively on fish, for which it dives to depths of twenty metres.

Its closest American relative is the great cormorant *(Phalacrocorax carbo).*

Length:
76 cm.
The male and female have like plumage. In the breeding season it has a short crest.
Voice:
Usual note a loud, rasping croak.
Size of Egg:
56.6 — 74.6
× 34.9 — 41.7 mm.

White Pelican

Pelecanus onocrotalus

Length:
140 to 178 cm.
The male and
female have like
plumage. Young
birds are
brownish.
Voice:
Bellowing sounds.
Size of Egg:
80.0 — 104.0
× 52.0 — 64.5 mm.

In Europe the white pelican still breeds in the Danube delta by the Black Sea. It is found along coastal lagoons, river deltas as well as large inland lakes. It is a dispersive as well as a migratory bird. After the breeding season it roams west as far as France and north as far as Sweden and Finland. In the Danube delta it was once very plentiful but today large aggregations no longer exist and colonies number several hundred birds at the most. The white pelican leaves its breeding grounds in September or October, wintering primarily in Egypt and the Middle East, and returning again between the end of March and May. The large nest of reeds and twigs is located in shallows amidst the tangle of reeds, which make access difficult. The birds usually start sitting on the nest a few days before the first egg is laid. The female usually lays one or two, sometimes three eggs in April to June, the partners taking turns to sit on the nest for twenty-nine to thirty-two days. Both also share the duties of feeding the young. When they are five weeks old the young begin to swim about in the vicinity of the nest, at the age of twelve weeks they take to the air, and at the age of fourteen to fifteen weeks they are fully able to fend for themselves. The white pelican often fishes in flocks with the birds forming a semi-circle and driving the fish to the shallows where they are more easily caught; it never dives. It feeds on various fish weighing 1.5 kilograms or less and will swallow even a stray duckling. In flight the head is drawn back and the neck held in a S-shape like that of herons.

Its closest American relative is also called the white pelican *(Pelecanus erythrorhynchos)*.

Dalmatian Pelican
Pelecanus crispus

Pelecanidae

The Dalmatian pelican is widespread in south-eastern Europe where it breeds in Bulgaria, Rumania, Yugoslavia and Greece. It occurs in greater numbers only in the Danube delta; populations in this area are migrant. In winter it travels mostly to the Nile in North Africa, leaving its nesting grounds in late August and returning again in March. The birds usually begin building the nest about a week after their arrival. The male brings material in his beak, delivering it to the female on the water beside the nest. This is generally located on flattened reeds or other vegetation and always in shallows. In large colonies the nests are often packed closely side by side. Between the end of March and beginning of May, the female lays two eggs as a rule, which both partners take turns incubating, beginning as soon as the first is laid. The young generally hatch after thirty to thirty-two days. At first they are fed food regurgitated by the parents into the nest, when older they thrust their heads into the parents' pouches. They are able to fly at the age of twelve weeks but are not fully independent until they are fourteen to fifteen weeks old. The diet consists solely of fish for which the birds forage in groups, often in coastal inlets as well as in the open sea.

Its closest American relative is the white pelican *(Pelecanus erythrorhynchos).*

Length:
171 cm.
The male and female have like plumage.
Voice:
Bellowing notes such as 'wo-wo-wo', 'kh-kh-kh'.
Size of Egg:
78.0 — 106.0 × 53.0 — 64.0 mm.

Little Egret
Egretta garzetta

The little egret is widely distributed in Africa and Asia. In Europe it breeds in Spain, southern Portugal, southern France and the Balkan peninsula. It is found mostly in river deltas, lagoons and marshes, but also occurs inland. A migrant bird, it frequently strays into central and western Europe. European birds winter in Africa south as far as the Cape of Good Hope and also in southern Asia. It departs from its breeding grounds in late August or September, from areas farther south as late as November or December. It comes back again between mid-March and May, in southern France as early as February. The little egret nests in colonies, often together with other herons. The nest is placed in bushes or on trees, sometimes even in forests. There may be over twenty nests on a single tree, often only seventy-five centimetres apart. Made of sticks and reeds, they are built by both partners soon after the birds' arrival. The female usually lays three to six eggs in May or June, which both partners take turns incubating, beginning as soon as the first egg is laid with the result that the young hatch in succession. The period of incubation is twenty-one to twenty-five days. The young are fed by both parents who fly in search of food often as far as twenty kilometres from the nesting site. The diet consists of small fish, amphibians, worms, crustaceans and insects, on rare occasions also small songbirds.

A closely related American species is the snowy egret *(Leucophoyx thula).*

Length:
56 cm.
The male and female have like plumage.
Voice:
A croaking 'kark'.
Size of Egg:
41.1 — 55.0
× 30.0 — 38.0 mm.

Greater Flamingo — American Flamingo

Phoenicopterus ruber

Phoenicopteridae

In Europe the greater flamingo breeds in southern France in the Rhône delta in the Camargue, and in southern Spain. It usually migrates to North Africa and the Mediterranean, some birds, however, remaining and roaming the countryside in the vicinity of the breeding area. Single individuals may occasionally be met with in Great Britain, central Europe and as far north as Norway and Finland. The greater flamingo inhabits coastal lagoons, shallow lakes and in Africa also inland salt lakes. Birds nesting in Russia fly regularly to the Danube delta where they may be found in shallow lagoons near the shore. This flamingo nests in colonies, often in large numbers, with an average of two nests to a square metre. These are placed either on shallow water or on the shore near water. Shaped like a chimney twenty to fifty centimetres high, they are made of mud or sand reinforced with small twigs and feathers. The birds use their bills to construct the nest, which they then tread down with their feet, hollowing out a shallow depression in the top with their beaks in which the female lays her single egg (sometimes two or three). As a rule she incubates by herself for a period of thirty to thirty-two days. On hatching the chicks remain in the nest for four days (sometimes more), after which they form small groups and wade in the shallows. The adult birds feed their offspring a sort of thick soup for three weeks after which the young birds forage for themselves, though the parents bring them food for another two to three weeks. The diet consists mainly of small crustaceans, also molluscs, worms, aquatic insects and the like as well as plant food.

Length:
127 cm.
The male and female have like plumage. The young bird is brownish.
Voice:
Resembling the cackling of geese. In flight also 'ar-honk'.
Size of Egg:
77.0 — 103.5 × 47.7 — 60.1 mm.
The eggs are white.

Whooper Swan

Cygnus cygnus

Anatidae

The whooper swan is found in northern Scotland, northern Scandinavia and Finland, northern Russia and Iceland. It also breeds in northern Asia. Its wintering grounds embrace practically the whole of Europe but in winter it is found mostly along the coasts of Iceland, Great Britain, Ireland, southern Scandinavia, Germany, Holland and the coasts of the Black and Caspian Seas. It may be seen inland on ice-free rivers only in severe winters, as a rule, and in small flocks. During the breeding season it is found in coastal waters, river deltas, as well as lakes and large rivers in the arctic tundra. It prefers still bodies of water with beds of reeds. The nest, placed on islands or in swamps, is usually a large mass of reeds and other vegetation; the hollow is lined with down. The female lays three to six eggs and does not begin incubating until three days after the last is laid. She incubates by herself while the male stands guard close by. The chicks hatch after thirty-five to forty days and as soon as they have dried are led by the parents out on the water. They are covered with a lovely pinkish down at first; by the age of two months this coat is replaced by feathers coloured a dingy grey, thus making it easy to distinguish the young from the adult birds, which are white. The whooper swan feeds almost exclusively on vegetable matter: grass, green shoots and various seeds. The young, however, also eat animal food such as various aquatic insects and their larvae.

A closely related American species is the trumpeter swan *(Olor buccinator)*.

Length:
152 cm.
The male and female have like plumage.
Voice:
Loud, bugle-like whooping sounds.
Size of Egg:
104.5 — 126.3
× 68.0 — 77.4 mm.

Bewick's Swan — Whistling Swan

Cygnus bewickii

Anatidae

Bewick's swan is found in the northern Asiatic tundras of Russia as well as in European tundras. Besides being smaller than the whooper swan it also differs from the latter in the extent of yellow colouring on the bill which is restricted only to the area above the nostrils. Its regular wintering grounds are the North Sea region, England and Ireland, where in some places it occurs in huge flocks numbering thousands of birds. It winters in smaller numbers along the coast of the Baltic Sea and also makes its way as far as the Black and Caspian Seas. It leaves its northern breeding grounds at the beginning of October, returning again in early April. It nests in swampy tundras near the seacoast, preferring country with shallow lakes and streams. The nest is placed on an elevated spot near water. Built solely by the female, it is made of moss, lichens and other vegetation growing in the vicinity and is lined with fine down. The eggs, usually three or four, are laid in the second half of June and are incubated by the female for thirty-four to thirty-eight days while the male stands guard close by. Bewick's swan eats mostly plant food and also in small quantities aquatic insects and their larvae, occasionally also a small fish or tadpole.

Length:
122 cm.
The male and female have like plumage.
Voice:
Bugle-like, musical notes.
Size of Egg:
96.0 — 114.0 × 64.3 — 71.7 mm.

Bean Goose
Anser fabalis

Anatidae

The bean goose is found mostly in the southern arctic tundras. In Europe it breeds in Iceland, northern Scandinavia, Finland and northern Russia. European populations winter in western and southern Europe, in the coastal regions of southern and central Scandinavia and on the coasts of the Black Sea. However, it also winters on pastures close to inland bodies of water. It associates to form large flocks in the winter months. The night is usually spent on bare islands without any tall vegetation or on the open water of lakes and ponds. When grazing several geese stand guard while the others feed. They fly in search of food after sunset and usually spend the day resting. The bean goose arrives at its breeding grounds in May. It prefers the edges of lakes and rivers but also nests in moorland and on the rocky banks of mountain streams. The female starts preparing the nest in a shallow depression under a bush or low tree soon after the birds' arrival, lining it with vegetation and down. The three to seven eggs are usually laid in June and are incubated by the female alone for twenty-seven to thirty days while her mate stands guard close by. When danger threatens both birds crouch on the ground with their necks outstretched. They leave their breeding grounds in flocks at the end of August or beginning of September, birds inhabiting more southerly areas leave as late as October. The diet consists of grass, shoots and berries and in the autumn mostly of seeds. The small, downy goslings and adult birds in moult also eat insects.

Its closest American relative is the snow goose (*Chen hyperborea*).

Length:
71 to 89 cm.
The male and female have like plumage.
Voice:
Low, honking notes such as 'ung-unk'.
Size of Egg:
74.0 — 91.0
× 42.0 — 59.0 mm.

White-fronted Goose
Anser albifrons

Anatidae

In Europe the white-fronted goose breeds only in
the northern part of Russia bordering the sea; it
is also found in northern Asia, northern North
America and on the eastern coast of Greenland.
It winters on the coasts of western Europe, Great
Britain and Ireland as well as in eastern Scandinavia and on the Black Sea. It occasionally occurs as a vagrant deep inside central Europe. It
returns to its breeding grounds from mid-May
onwards, but if they are located in mountain areas then not until mid-June. It frequently nests in
small colonies. It inhabits treeless tundras and
open moorland near the sea, also islands in river
deltas and slopes on the edges of rivers and lakes.
The nest is placed in an elevated spot, often on
terraced hillsides. The hollow is lined with various kinds of vegetation and from the start of
incubation also with a thick layer of down. It is
not unusual for the nest to be located near that
of a peregrine falcon, because the raptor pro-
vides protection against attack by the arctic fox.
In late May, or more usually in June, the female
lays three to seven eggs, which she incubates by
herself for twenty-six to thirty days. The male
remains beside the nest or nearby throughout the
entire period. When the young are grown families join to form flocks that may be found on wet
pastures with rich vegetation alongside rivers
and lakes. The white-fronted goose feeds on
grass, shoots, various berries and also seeds.

Length:
66 to 76 cm.
The male and
female have like
plumage.
Voice:
High-pitched
notes such as
'lyo-lyok',
'kow-lyow' and
the like.
Size of Egg:
72.0 — 89.6
× 46.7 — 59.0 mm.

Lesser White-fronted Goose
Anser erythropus

Anatidae

The lesser white-fronted goose is at home in the coastal tundras of Europe and Asia. In Europe it breeds in northern Scandinavia, Finland and northern Russia. Winter is spent in southeastern Europe on the coasts of the Black and Caspian Seas, occasionally also on the coasts of the Baltic and North Seas. Single individuals may occur as vagrants in the interior, usually during migration. In central Europe it may be met with from September to November and again from March to early May on its return flight to its breeding grounds, where it arrives at the end of May or beginning of June. The geese roam the countryside in flocks until all traces of snow have disappeared, after which they break up into individual pairs that establish their separate nests in a concealed spot under bushes. The four to five eggs are laid in late June and the beginning of July and are incubated by the female alone for twenty-six to twenty-seven days while the male remains nearby to warn her of any approaching danger. When the young are grown the geese form large flocks. In July, during the moult, they are often to be seen on land and when danger threatens they make their escape by running away on foot at great speed. The lesser white-fronted goose forages for food only on land; it eats grass, leaves, shoots and berries.

Its closest American relative is the white-fronted goose *(Anser albifrons)*.

Length:
53 to 56 cm.
The male and female have like plumage.
Voice:
The male's high-pitched 'kyn-yn' or 'kyn-yn-yn' the female's a 'kow-yow'.
Size of Egg:
69.0—84.5
× 43.0—52.0 mm.

Canada Goose
Branta canadensis

Anatidae

The original home of the Canada goose is North America. Since the seventeenth century, however, it has been raised in a semi-wild state in England and also in Sweden, where it was later let loose and went wild, thus giving rise to the European populations. British birds are resident, whereas birds nesting in southern Sweden depart in winter for the coasts of Germany and Holland, occurring at times as vagrants even in other European countries, though these may be escapes from zoos. In winter the Canada goose is found mostly by the coast. It breeds in coastal marshes as well as inland on pastures beside water and sometimes also in open woodlands with lakes and ponds. The nest is located on small islands or in swamps. The hollow is lined with dry leaves, grass and other vegetation and the eggs are covered with down. The five to six eggs are laid in early April and are incubated by the female alone for twenty-eight to twenty-nine days, while the male keeps careful watch close by. When the young are grown, families join to form flocks that roam the countryside. As a rule they forage for food on dry land, mostly in the early morning or at dusk. The diet consists of grass, grain, shoots, berries and seeds, occasionally also insects, their larvae, and molluscs.

Length:
Male 99 cm,
female 93.5 cm.
The male and
female have like
plumage.
Voice:
A hoarse honking
that sounds like
'aa-honk'.
Size of Egg:
79.0 — 99.0
× 53.5 — 64.5 mm.

Barnacle Goose
Branta leucopsis

The range of the barnacle goose embraces the north Atlantic from the eastern coast of Greenland through Spitsbergen to the south of Novaya Zemlya. It winters on the coasts of Ireland, England, northern France, Holland, West Germany and Denmark. Individual flocks wander as far as the Mediterranean, to the Azores and the eastern coast of North America. Birds begin migrating in late August or early September. Single individuals from Spitsbergen fly to their wintering grounds and back across the open sea and along the coast of Scandinavia, Greenland populations fly across Iceland and Novaya Zemlya populations fly across the Baltic Sea. The barnacle goose nests in colonies on the seacoast as well as alongside rivers, often near the nests of raptors, which serve to protect them from the arctic fox. It arrives at its breeding grounds in the second half of May. The nest is located on steep cliffs as high as fifty metres above the sea, often in colonies of guillemots, kittiwakes and other seabirds. The female lays three to five, sometimes as many as seven eggs, usually in the second half of June, incubating them by herself for twenty-four to twenty-six days. When they have dried out the goslings leap from the cliffs into the water. During the nesting season the barnacle goose feeds mainly on coastal vegetation, shoots and the like, in winter on grass, aquatic plants, seaweeds and occasionally also on crustaceans, molluscs and aquatic insects.

Length:
58 to 69 cm.
The male and female have like plumage.
Voice:
Usually rapid, repeated barks that sound like 'gnuk'.
Size of Egg:
68.0—82.7 × 46.0—54.0 mm.

Brent Goose — Brant Goose

Branta bernicla

Anatidae

The brent goose inhabits the tundras of northern Asia and North America; in Europe it breeds only on islands off the north coast of Russia. It is a sea and coastal bird. In Europe it winters chiefly on the coast of Denmark and West Germany, and less often on the coast of East Germany, Holland, Belgium, France, England and Ireland. It returns to its breeding grounds in the first half of June, whereupon it immediately sets about preparing its nest — a hollow, not very deep, lined with vegetation and down. The brent goose nests in small colonies in dry, elevated places. In June the female lays three to six, sometimes eight eggs, which she incubates by herself for twenty-four to twenty-six days. It is interesting to note that the males abandon their families very early to form small flocks of their own sex. The complete summer moult begins in mid-July, the new flight feathers being fully grown-in between about the 10th and 15th of August. At this time the young are also already able to fly but have not as yet acquired their full plumage. In winter the brent goose feeds on marine vegetation, in summer on grass, lichens, moss and the like, as well as crustaceans, molluscs, aquatic insects and their larvae, and other invertebrates. The brent goose is now becoming increasingly scarce. Up to about 1930 some ten thousand of these birds wintered in Holland alone, whereas since 1953 their number has barely totalled one thousand, the same being true in other wintering grounds.

Length:
56 to 61 cm.
The male and female have like plumage.
Voice:
Guttural sounds such as 'rronk' or 'rruk'.
Size of Egg:
51.0 — 81.1
× 36.5 — 66.0 mm

Shelduck
Tadorna tadorna

The shelduck is at home on the coasts of Ireland, England, Scandinavia, Denmark, Germany, Holland, France and the Black Sea coast. Its distribution extends as far as central China and Afghanistan. In Asia it is also found on salt lakes. It winters throughout all of western and southern Europe as well as in North Africa. During migration it occasionally occurs as a vagrant on inland ponds and large rivers. In more southerly parts of its range it is resident, its favourite habitats being sandy shores, mudflats or islands, often near colonies of gulls and terns. It is fond of nesting in burrows, e.g. abandoned fox holes, but will also lay its eggs amidst a pile of stones or in a rock cavity. The nesting hollow is only sparingly lined, either with leaves or pieces of wood or more often merely with down. In May to June the female lays seven to twelve, sometimes as many as twenty eggs, which she incubates by herself for twenty-seven to twenty-nine days. During this period the male remains close by on the lookout for any threat of danger. The newly hatched ducklings are led out on the water by their mother as soon as they have dried out. The shelduck feeds on marine molluscs, crustaceans, worms, aquatic insects and their larvae, partly also on plant food and on occasion even fish spawn or tadpoles.

It has no close American relative.

Length:
61 cm.
The female is not as brightly coloured. In the breeding season the drake has a large red knob at the base of the bill.
Voice:
A characteristic rapid call 'ak-ak-ak' also 'ark, ark'.
Size of Egg:
61.1—71.0 × 42.0—51.0 mm.

Scaup — Greater Scaup

Aythya marila

The scaup, a small diving duck, is at home in the extreme northern parts of Europe, northern Asia, Canada and Alaska. In Europe it breeds in northern Scandinavia, Murmansk and Iceland. Outside the breeding season it spends practically all its time on the sea or in river deltas. A migrant, it winters in flocks sometimes numbering thousands of birds along the coasts of western Europe, Great Britain, southern Scandinavia, Germany, Denmark and Poland, as well as in Italy and the areas round the Black and Caspian Seas. It returns to its breeding grounds — still bodies of water in the tundra or moors — in late April, exhibiting a fondness for localities close to the nesting sites of gulls and terns. The nest is generally located on dry land close to the water's edge and is lined with a thick layer of down. The scaup often nests in colonies. In May to June the female lays six to nine, sometimes as many as twelve eggs, which she incubates by herself for twenty-four to twenty-eight days, leading the newly-hatched ducklings out onto the water as soon as they have dried out. At first the ducklings feed on insects which they capture on vegetation or on the water. Adult birds feed mostly on molluscs, small crustaceans, worms and insects, and will sometimes also eat small fish. Seeds and aquatic vegetation form only a small part of their diet.

Length:
48 cm.
Sexual dimorphism.
Voice:
The male's a whistling note, the female's a low 'karr-karr'.
Size of Egg:
54.5 — 68.3 × 39.0 — 48.0 mm.

Eider — Common Eider

Somateria mollissima

Anatidae

In Europe the eider is found along the coast of Iceland, in all of Scandinavia, Finland, the Murmansk region, Scotland, Ireland, Denmark and the islands of West Germany and Holland. It also makes its home in northern Asia and northern North America. Birds inhabiting the extreme northern parts of the range are migrant, but otherwise the eider is either a partial migrant or resident. In winter it occurs in large flocks along the coast of western Europe and the North and Baltic Seas. Single young individuals may occur as vagrants in the heart of central Europe. The eider nests in colonies often numbering a hundred or even a thousand pairs. It is protected by law in practically all parts of its range and therefore exhibits no fear of man. The nest is located among rocks, under pieces of wood, under bushes and such like and is lined with small twigs, leaves, seaweed or only small pebbles. After the eggs are laid a great quantity of soft eiderdown is added. The female lays three to nine eggs, young females, however, only two or three. She incubates by herself for twenty-five to twenty-eight days and within five to ten hours after the ducklings have hatched she leads them to water, which is often as much as one-and-a-half kilometres from the nest. The young birds are already capable of flight at the age of sixty to seventy-five days and are fully grown by the time they are eighty to ninety days old. The mainstay of the diet is molluscs, mostly mussels and cockles, but the eider also eats crustaceans, worms, starfish and fish. It usually dives to depths of about six metres in pursuit of its prey.

Length:
58 cm.
Marked sexual dimorphism.
Voice:
The male's a ringing 'coo-roo-uh', the female's a quacking 'korr-r'.
Size of Egg:
68.0 — 88.0 × 46.7 — 56.5 mm.

Common Scoter

Melanitta nigra

The common scoter is at home in northern Europe, northern Asia and western Alaska. In Europe it breeds in Iceland, central and northern Scandinavia, northern Finland, in the coastal regions of Russia, in Scotland and in Ireland. Outside the breeding season it spends all its time at sea. Some populations are resident, others migrant. In winter larger groups may be found along the entire coast of western Europe, Great Britain, the North and Baltic Seas and to some extent also the coast of northwest Africa. The birds return to their nesting grounds on lakes, moors and tundras in May. The nest is located near water in tall grass, under bushes, among rocks and the like, and is lined sparingly by the female with moss, lichens or dry grass. The clutch usually consists of five to eight eggs which the female begins incubating in June, shortly after which the male abandons his mate. The young hatch after twenty-seven to thirty-one days and are led to water by their mother as soon as they have dried. They remain in her company for six to seven weeks after which they fend for themselves, though they stay in flocks. The scoter obtains its food only by diving, usually to depths of about six metres. It feeds on molluscs, crustaceans, worms, and in the breeding grounds also on aquatic insects and their larvae. Its diet likewise includes vegetable matter such as the green parts of aquatic plants. When pursued by a bird of prey it makes its escape by diving into the water from the air.

Length:
48 cm.
Sexual
dimorphism.
Voice:
The male's
a ringing call, the
female's various
rasping sounds.
Size of Egg:
59.0 — 72.0
× 41.3 — 47.7 mm

Velvet Scoter — White-winged Scoter

Melanitta fusca

Anatidae

In Europe the velvet scoter is found in Scandinavia, Finland, northwest Russia and Scotland, also in northern Asia eastward as far as Kamchatka as well as in North America. Mostly a migratory bird, it winters mainly along the coasts of western Europe, the North Sea and Baltic Sea and also in the southern part of the Black Sea. In winter it may by encountered fairly regularly on inland lakes, ponds, and rivers. The birds arrive at their breeding grounds, already paired, in late April or early May. They nest along seashores and on islands, as well as on inland bodies of water in the tundra and taiga and in Scandinavia also in mountain areas. The nest is located in tall grass, under bushes, among rocks, usually near water. It is merely a depression lined sparingly with bits of leaves, grass, pine needles and such like but with a thick layer of down. Between the end of May and beginning of June the female lays six to ten, sometimes even as many as fourteen eggs, which she incubates by herself for twenty-eight to thirty days. After the ducklings have hatched she remains together with them on the water. The diet consists of small crustaceans, molluscs, the larvae of aquatic insects and also small bits of green aquatic vegetation. Adult birds obtain food solely by diving for it to depths of two to five metres.

Length:
56 cm.
Sexual dimorphism.
Voice:
The male's a whistling note 'kiu' or 'whur-er', the female's harsh, rasping sounds.
Size of Egg:
64.3 — 77.5
× 42.6 — 51.5 mm.

♀

♂

Goldeneye — Common Goldeneye

Bucephala clangula

Anatidae

The goldeneye is found throughout northern Europe and in central Europe in the Bohemian part of Czechoslovakia and Switzerland. It winters in western, central, southern and southeastern Europe on lakes, ponds and rivers, even in cities. The nest is generally located right by the water. The birds begin pairing in their wintering grounds and continue courting in their breeding territories, where they return as soon as the ice thaws. The female seeks out the nesting cavity, followed then by the male. The cavity is often one used the previous year but it may be a new one as well. Tree holes chosen for a nesting site are usually 2.5 to 5 metres above the ground. Often the nest is sited in an old nest hole of the black woodpecker. In April to May the female lays six to eleven eggs in the bottom of the cavity, which she only rarely lines with bits of moss. However, the eggs are surrounded with soft down. The female incubates by herself for twenty-seven to thirty-two days. When the newly hatched ducklings have dried out they jump out of the nest, usually landing in soft grass or water unharmed. Food is obtained mostly in the water and consists of insects and their larvae, worms, molluscs, crustaceans as well as small fish and to a lesser extent green vegetation and seeds. The goldeneye dives to depths of as much as nine metres.

Length:
46 cm.
Sexual dimorphism.
Voice:
The male utters sounds like 'qui-rrik', when courting 'rrrr', the female's is usually a low-pitched 'grarr grarr'.
Size of Egg:
52.0 — 68.0
× 39.4 — 47.0 mm.

Red-breasted Merganser

Mergus serrator

Anatidae

In Europe the red-breasted merganser is at home in Iceland, Scotland, northwest England, Scandinavia, Finland and Russia. In central Europe it breeds regularly along the shores of Germany, Poland and Denmark and in rare instances Holland. It is also found in northern Asia, North America and Greenland. Outside the breeding season it spends most of its time at sea, being encountered inland only in its flights across land. In the southern parts of its range it is resident or a partial migrant, in the more northern parts it is migrant. In early May, about two to three weeks before laying eggs, the female begins seeking a suitable site for the nest. The male follows his mate or else waits for her on the water by the shore. The nest is built by the female alone in dense clumps of grass or other vegetation, under bushes, among rocks, between the roots of trees as well as in holes in the ground, but always on dry land. It is usually located near water, but sometimes may be as much as a hundred metres from the water's edge, and is lined with dry as well as green vegetation from the neighbourhood. At the end of May and in June, occasionally as late as July, the female lays five to twelve eggs which she incubates by herself for twenty-eight to thirty-two days. During this period the male remains close by on the water. The newly hatched young are taken out on the water by their mother as soon as they have dried out; they are able to fly at the age of fifty-nine days. The diet consists of small fish, molluscs, crustaceans, aquatic insects and worms.

Length:
Male — 59.5 cm,
female — 52 cm.
Sexual
dimorphism.
Voice:
The male has
a rasping
disyllabic
courtship note;
the female's
generally
'rock-rock-rock'.
Size of Egg:
56.5 — 70.7
× 40.3 — 47.6 mm.

Goosander — Common Merganser

Anatidae

Mergus merganser

The goosander inhabits a large territory ranging from Iceland and the British Isles eastwards through northern Europe and the northern part of central Asia as far as northern China and Sakhalin. On rare occasions it also breeds in the Swiss Alps, also widely in North America. It is either resident or a partial migrant; in the northerly parts of its range, however, it is migrant. In winter it is often encountered on inland rivers. It nests chiefly on inland bodies of water which are unpolluted, sufficiently deep and are bordered by old trees. In spring the female seeks a suitable nesting cavity in old, usually broad-leaved trees, though the nest may also be located in rock cavities. In trees the nest is sited some 2.5 to 18 metres above the ground, on cliffs as high as fifty metres above the water. In cavities the eggs are laid on the bare surface, whereas in open nests the hollow is usually lined with grass, leaves and moss. Between mid-March and May, when the clutch is complete (seven to twelve eggs), the female begins incubating. The young hatch after twenty-eight to thirty-two days, whereupon they jump out of the nest into the water, where they swim about with their mother. The goosander feeds mainly on fish but also eats crustaceans and other small animal life it finds in water. It can dive into water from the air. Eels, salmon and fish of that ilk are its favourite prey.

Length:
Male — 75.5 cm, female — 57.5 cm. Sexual dimorphism.
Voice:
The male's low-pitched, croaking sounds, the female's sounds like 'karr'.
Size of Egg:
55.4—74.5 × 37.0—50.0 mm.

White-tailed Eagle or Sea Eagle

Haliaeetus albicilla

Accipitridae

The white-tailed eagle inhabits the northern and eastern coasts of Scandinavia, Iceland, the eastern part of central Europe, northeastern and southeastern Europe and also northern and central Asia and southwestern Greenland. In autumn and winter it is regularly encountered in central Europe. It nests on rocky coasts or large inland bodies of water as well as water courses. It shows up at its central European breeding grounds as early as January or February and immediately sets about building its nest — a huge structure placed in a tall tree or on a cliff ledge, in rare instances even on the ground. It is made of a mass of sticks and branches, and though large, the actual nesting hollow is small. The same nest is used for years in succession, being added on to every year and sometimes measuring as much as two metres across and 1¹/₂ metres in height. In February to April the female lays two to three eggs, sometimes only one, which both partners take turns incubating for thirty-one to forty-six days. The young are fed fish and small waterfowl by the parents. They abandon the nest after fifty to seventy-seven days. The mainstay of the diet is fish and birds, mainly coots. An experienced eagle will capture even a goose or heron, but young birds are not as skilled and often will eat dead fish that have been washed ashore. The white-tailed eagle plucks its prey out of the water with its talons; only rarely does it plunge into the water in a steep dive.

A closely related American species is the bald eagle *(Haliaeetus leucocephalus).*

Length:
69 to 91 cm.
The female is somewhat larger than the male.
Wingspan:
Up to 240 cm.
Weight:
4 to 6 kg.
Voice:
A clear 'kri, kri, kri', also a low-pitched 'kra'.
Size of Egg:
66.0—84.8 × 53.0—63.5 mm.
The eggs are pure white.

Gyrfalcon
Falco rusticolus

Falconidae

The gyrfalcon is a bird of the arctic tundras, and also inhabits the mountains of central Asia, the arctic region of North America and Greenland. In Europe it breeds in Iceland and along the coast of northern Scandinavia. It is found in open rocky locations, on the seacoast and on islands, locally also on the edges of coniferous forests. Some birds are resident, some migrate south or southeast, but not too far from their breeding grounds. Only very occasionally does the gyrfalcon stray into central or western Europe. It occurs in a number of colour phases. There are two basic colour forms — one white and the other greyish brown. The white form is found in Greenland. There is, of course, a great range of colour variations between the two extremes. The gyrfalcon builds its nest on rocky ledges, preferably near colonies of waterfowl, which provide it with a rich source of food. However, it also nests in tall trees at a height of more than five metres and may occasionally site its nest on the edges of rivers. The nest is constructed of birch or willow twigs or the twigs of the tree it happens to be located in, and the hollow is lined with dry grass, willow leaves as well as food remnants. The three to four eggs are laid between mid-April and the beginning of May and are incubated alternately by both partners for twenty-eight days. After forty-seven days in the nest the young venture forth for the first time. The spot where the adult birds pluck their prey clean is usually located 100 to 150 metres from the nest. The gyrfalcon hunts mostly waterfowl, also corvine birds and ptarmigan, on rare occasions even small mammals.

Length:
51 to 56 cm.
The male and female have like plumage.
Voice:
High-pitched barking sounds.
Size of Egg:
48.4 — 64.5
× 36.5 — 54.6 mm.

Oystercatcher — American Oystercatcher

Haematopus ostralegus

Haematopodidae

The oystercatcher is found practically throughout the whole world. In Europe it may be seen almost everywhere on the coast. Birds inhabiting the area south of the British Isles and Denmark are resident, those from more northern parts are usually migrant, wintering in southern Europe and along the coast of North Africa. North of the Black Sea and in central Asia it also breeds on shallow, inland salt lakes. Outside the breeding season it runs about in groups in shallows, on mudflats or sandy beaches seeking food. Spring is the time of the courtship display during which several birds run beside or behind one another constantly uttering loud piping trills. Paired birds then stake out their nesting territories, which are not very big but which they courageously defend against all intruders. The nest is a shallow scrape in the ground, usually on the shore near water, lined with small shells or shell fragments, also leaves or grass. Both partners take turns incubating the two to four eggs. The young hatch after twenty-six to twenty-eight days and remain in the hollow for one or two days after which they roam the neighbourhood with their parents. At first they are brought food by the adult birds but very soon they gather it themselves. The diet consists of molluscs, worms, insects and such like. The birds often probe deep in the mud and sand with their long bills to catch small invertebrates; often they extract the animals from seashells and are skilful at opening the shells of bivalves.

Length:
43 cm.
The male and female have like plumage.
Voice:
A loud 'pic, pic, pic', when courting, piping trills.
Size of Egg:
47.7 — 70.1
× 32.8 — 48.9 mm.

Ringed Plover
Charadrius hiaticula

The ringed plover is a bird of sandy and muddy localities on the seacoast. In Europe it breeds in Scandinavia, Finland, Russia, Iceland, Great Britain, Germany, Denmark, Holland, Belgium and France. On occasion it also nests on the shores of inland lakes and ponds in central Europe. British birds are mostly resident, those from other areas migrate south, wintering chiefly in southeastern Europe and North Africa. During the spring and autumn migration it may often be encountered on inland waters. It arrives at its nesting grounds in flocks in April or May, forming pairs shortly after. It is interesting to note that the females are the first to arrive; the males come after and this is followed by the courtship display. Paired birds then establish their nesting territories, often the same ones as the previous year. The male makes several nests (shallow scrapes in the ground) for the female to choose from. They are usually located close to water, in sand or among rocks, and are lined with small stones or shell fragments. In May and June, sometimes also in July, the female lays four eggs which both partners take turns incubating for twenty-three to twenty-six days. The newly-hatched young abandon the nest as soon as they have dried and are tended by their parents. When they are able to fly they roam the countryside in small flocks. The females are again the first to depart when it is time for the autumn flight. The ringed plover feeds mainly on insects and their larvae, also worms, small crustaceans and molluscs.

Length:
19 cm.
The male and female have like plumage.
Voice:
A mellow call that sounds like 'too-li', when courting, a repeated 'quitu-weeoo'.
Size of Egg:
32.0 — 39.6 × 22.8 — 28.5 mm.

Kentish Plover — Snowy Plover

Charadrius alexandrinus

Charadriidae

The Kentish plover is found mainly on the seashore from East Germany along the western coast of Europe, the southern and southeastern coast, the coasts of the Black and Caspian Seas and in the Danube delta. It also occurs in Africa, Asia, Australia and America, occasionally even on inland salt lakes. Birds inhabiting southern regions are resident, those in more northerly localities migrate to southern Europe and North Africa. The first half of April is when most birds arrive at their breeding grounds. The nesting territory is selected and staked out by the male, who also prepares the nest. It is usually a shallow depression in the sand lined with small pebbles, bits of wood and grass. Often these birds nest in colonies, sometimes together with the little tern. In open sandy locations a strong wind sometimes covers the whole clutch with sand. A full clutch, i.e. three eggs, may be found in the nest in May or June, occasionally as early as late April and sometimes as late as July. If the eggs are lost the birds make a new nest and the female lays a new clutch of eggs, often within a week's time. Both partners take turns incubating for twenty-four to twenty-eight days. By the time they are forty days old the young are able to fly and they then roam the coastline in small flocks looking for food. The diet consists of small crustaceans, molluscs, insects and their larvae. On wet sands and mudflats these birds may be seen pattering about, their stamping feet stirring up the concealed invertebrates which they then eat.

Length:
16 cm.
The male and female have like plumage.
Voice:
Delicate sounds such as 'wit-wit-wit', a flute-like 'poo-eef'. When courting, trills such as 'tritritritritrirr'.
Size of Egg:
30.1 — 35.4 × 22.1 — 25.2 mm.

Golden Plover
Pluvialis apricaria

Charadriidae

The golden plover is found in Iceland, Scandinavia, Finland, Great Britain, Ireland and northern Russia. It breeds locally in Denmark, West Germany and Holland. Two subspecies are known — the northern and the southern, which differs from the former in that it lacks the black cheeks and also the broad black band on the flanks and belly. In their eclipse plumage, i.e. in winter, the two forms are alike. British birds are resident, whereas birds from the north migrate across central Europe in large numbers in the autumn (and spring) on their way to (and back from) their wintering grounds in southern Europe, North Africa and the Middle East. At this time small flocks of these birds may be seen in fields. After their arrival at the breeding grounds in open marshlands and moors in late March and April the flocks disband to form pairs, which settle in their nesting territories. The nest is a hollow in the ground lined with plant stems, leaves, small twigs and the like. The female lays four eggs as a rule, which she incubates alone, relieved now and then by the male. Her mate, however, remains on guard close by, warning the female of approaching danger and then trying to distract the intruder and lead him away from the nest. The young usually hatch after twenty-seven days. The diet consists mostly of small invertebrates.

Its closest American relative is the American or lesser golden plover *(Pluvialis dominica)*.

Length:
28 cm.
The male and female have like plumage. The black coloration is absent in the winter plumage.
Voice:
A flute-like 'tlu-i', when courting, 'tirr-peeoo' and the like.
Size of Egg:
45.5 — 56.3
× 33.2 — 38.3 mm

Turnstone — Ruddy Turnstone
Arenaria interpres

Charadriidae

The turnstone is at home on the coasts of Scandinavia and Finland as well as northern Siberia, arctic North America and Greenland. During the migrating season it may be encountered practically throughout the whole of Europe, but it winters on the coasts of western and southwestern Europe and North Africa. Some individuals fly as far as Australia and South America. The birds leave their breeding grounds as early as the end of July but more usually in August or September, returning again in April or May, though birds from the extreme north often do not arrive there until early June. The turnstone inhabits rocky islands and shores in the arctic, also river islands. The nest is located near water. It is a shallow depression lined with dry vegetable matter. In May or June, in the far north often as late as July, the female lays her clutch of four eggs. The partners take turns incubating, but towards the end of this period the female often leaves the task to the male, who also cares for the young when they hatch, which is after twenty-three to twenty-four days. It has been discovered, however, that often the young are tended by both parents. When foraging for food the turnstone has the characteristic habit of turning small stones over with its bill to reveal hidden invertebrates, which it then eats. The diet consists of insects and their larvae, worms, small molluscs and also spiders.

Length:
23 cm.
The female is not as strikingly patterned as the male. In winter both sexes lose their rufous colouring.
Voice:
Abruptly uttered notes 'tuk-a tuk' or 'khikhikikikiki'.
Size of Egg:
36.0 — 44.6
× 26.0 — 31.3 mm.

Curlew or Whaup

Numenius arquata

Scolopacidae

The curlew is widely distributed along the coast of Scandinavia, in Great Britain, Ireland, western France, central, eastern and northeastern Europe as well as in northern and central Asia. A great many curlews winter in western Europe and along the coasts of the Mediterranean; some individuals, however, fly as far as eastern and southern Africa. West European populations are usually resident. During migration the curlew is often encountered on inland ponds and lakes and in recent years it has even begun to settle and breed in such places. The birds' typical habitats are moors, wet meadows, marshlands and also steppe areas with water. Late March is the time when the curlew returns to its breeding grounds. The nest is placed in tall grass or other vegetation. It is a hollow lined with dry grass, leaves or other vegetable matter, and is made by the male, who often prepares several such nests in the same area. In April or May the female usually lays four eggs which she and her partner take turns incubating for twenty-six to thirty days. The young birds are dry within twelve hours of hatching and then leave the nest, though they are protected by the parents as they forage for food. When the young are grown families join to form flocks. In the northern part of the curlew's range the females depart very early, sometimes abandoning the young when they are only ten days old and leaving them to the care of the male. The diet consists of worms, molluscs, spiders, insects and occasionally small tadpoles; the birds also nibble green plant parts, berries and seeds.

A closely related American species is the long-billed curlew *(Numenius americanus).*

Length:
53 to 58 cm.
The male and female have like plumage.
Voice:
A flute-like call such as 'cour-li' and the like which may be heard throughout the year.
Size of Egg:
56.2 — 78.6
× 41.7 — 55.1 mm.

Whimbrel
Numenius phaeopus

The whimbrel is found in northern Scandinavia, northern Finland, northern Russia, the Faroes and Scotland. Besides Europe it is also widespread in Siberia and North America. It is found on the seashore as well as inland on tundras, moors and wet meadows. It is a migratory bird which flies mainly along the coasts of Europe, sometimes also across central Europe and eastern populations across the Caspian Sea. It winters in northwestern, eastern and southern Africa, also in southern Asia, and occasionally along the coast of Spain. It leaves its breeding grounds often as early as late July but more often in August and September, at which time it occurs as a chance visitor in central Europe on the mud bottoms of drained ponds, on meadows and on fields near water. It returns to its nesting site again after mid-April and in May. The nest is a shallow hollow in the ground well concealed in a tussock of grass, heather or other vegetation and lined with grass, moss, lichens and the like. The female usually lays four eggs after mid-May or in June, sometimes even in July. Both partners incubate for about twenty-one to twenty-five days. The newly-hatched young leave the nest as soon as they are dry, remaining concealed in the surrounding vegetation where they are tended by the adult birds. The whimbrel feeds on insects and their larvae, worms, molluscs, spiders and other invertebrates. It also eats vegetable matter such as berries and seeds.

Length:
41 cm.
The male and female have like plumage.
Voice:
Flute-like notes.
Size of Egg:
52.0—65.1 × 36.0—45.0 mm.

Spotted Redshank
Tringa erythropus

Scolopacidae

The spotted redshank is found in northern Scandinavia and Finland, northern Russia and east as far as Kamchatka. North European populations winter mainly in the Mediterranean region and partly along the coast of western Europe. During migration, i.e. from August to October, small flocks of these birds may be regularly encountered inland in central Europe on the muddy shores of ponds and lakes. April and May is the time of the return flight but sometimes non-nesting birds may still be encountered in central Europe as late as June or July. The spotted redshank inhabits open localities such as on the edges of forests, on moors, and on meadows near water. The nest is a shallow depression lined sparingly with vegetation. The female usually lays four eggs in May and/or June, which both partners take turns incubating. The young hatch after three weeks and leave the nest as soon as they are dry, concealing themselves in clumps of grass, heather and the like in the vicinity. The parents tend their offspring until they are able to fend for themselves, after which the birds join with others to form flocks. Food is obtained in shallows in the mud, the birds often wading belly-deep in the water. When a strong wind is blowing the birds keep to the sheltered part of the shore, taking their prey from the incoming waves. The diet consists mainly of small molluscs and also aquatic insects.

A closely related American species is the lesser yellowlegs *(Totanus flavipes)*.

Length:
30.5 cm.
The male and female have like plumage.
Voice:
A loud 'tuinit', also 'chick-chick-chick'.
Size of Egg:
42.0−51.5
× 30.0−34.0 mm.

Greenshank
Tringa nebularia

right *Scolopacidae*

The greenshank is found in Scotland, western and northern Scandinavia, northern Finland and northern Russia. It winters throughout Africa and in southern Asia, but populations from eastern Asia may fly as far as Australia. Less commonly it winters no farther than southwestern Europe. During migration, from the end of July till the end of September and sometimes occasionally as late as November, it may be met with throughout Europe, even inland. It occurs in groups, often of about ten, rarely as many as forty birds. The greenshank returns to its breeding grounds again in April or May, the flight back taking less time than the autumn one. The breeding grounds are located in moors, heaths near water, treeless tundras and open woodlands. The nest is a shallow hollow lined with grass or other plant matter. In May or June the female usually lays four eggs, which she incubates mostly by herself, though the male occasionally relieves her. The young hatch after twenty-three to twenty-five days and, as soon as they are dry, scatter throughout the neighbourhood, concealing themselves in grass, heather, and the like. They are tended by the adult birds. The greenshank is one of the few waders to feed regularly on fish, which form about one-quarter of the bulk of its diet. When catching fish it immerses its entire head in the water. Besides this it also feeds on aquatic molluscs and insects, especially water boatmen.

Its closest American relative is the greater yellowlegs *(Totanus melanoleucus)*.

Length:
30.5 cm.
The male and female have like plumage.
Voice:
A loud 'tew-tew-tew', when courting, a flute-like 'tew-i'.
Size of Egg:
45.7 — 59.8 × 31.0 — 37.7 mm.

Wood Sandpiper

Tringa glareola

Scolopacidae

The wood sandpiper is widespread throughout Scandinavia, Finland, Scotland, northern Russia and in central Europe along the coasts of Poland and Germany. It migrates regularly through central Europe from late July to September and winters throughout practically all of Africa; eastern populations, however, fly to southern Asia and even as far as Australia. The birds return to their breeding grounds in April and May, though single non-nesting individuals may be met with in central and western Europe even in summer. The wood sandpiper is a small, active bird the size of a skylark and is constantly on the move. It inhabits open country in the northern tundra and along the northern coast, also the margins of open woodlands near water. The nest, lined only sparingly with grass, leaves of bushes and the like, is located in swamps, marshlands and marshy sites on the shore. The eggs, four as a rule, are laid in May or June, sometimes even in July, and are incubated by both partners for twenty-one to twenty-four days. The young remain in the nest for two days at the most, after which they wander about the neighbourhood foraging for food. When they are able to fly the birds roam the countryside in flocks and soon after depart for the wintering grounds. The diet consists of small invertebrates, especially water boatmen, the larvae of the harlequin fly and worms.

A closely related American species is the solitary sandpiper *(Tringa solitaria)*.

Length:
20 cm.
The male and female have like plumage.
Voice:
When courting, 'tleea-tleea-tleea', in flight a sharp 'chiff-iff-iff'.
Size of Egg:
33.0—42.5 × 24.4—29.3 mm.

Dunlin
Calidris alpina

Scolopacidae

The dunlin breeds along the coasts of Scandinavia, Finland, Russia, Poland, Germany, Denmark, Iceland, Great Britain and Ireland. European populations winter mostly on the coasts of western Europe and North Africa. During migration the dunlin is found throughout Europe on the muddy edges of ponds, lakes and rivers. Some birds, however, are resident. The dunlin is most numerous in the tundras. Late March and April is the time of its return to its breeding grounds. It is found on the seashore, river deltas as well as inland waters. Its characteristic habitat is a wet meadow, moor or marsh. The nest is located near water usually concealed by a tussock of grass. As a rule the female lays four eggs at the end of April or in May, in the extreme northern part of the dunlin's range as late as the beginning of June. Both partners take turns incubating for twenty-one to twenty-two days. As soon as the newly hatched birds are dry they leave the nest but remain in the neighbourhood. They are able to fly at the age of twenty-eight days, in the far northern tundras even by the time they are twenty days old. The birds then form flocks that roam the countryside seeking out water. At this time adult birds start migrating, whereas the young birds remain until the end of August. During migration the birds form huge flocks sometimes numbering several thousand individuals. They fly mainly at night. When the dunlin forages for food it wades in shallows but sometimes it also swims. During the nesting season the diet consists mainly of the larvae of mosquitoes and other insects, also small molluscs and crustaceans; in the autumn the birds gather seeds as well.

Length:
18 cm.
The male and female have like plumage.
Voice:
A high-pitched 'treer'; song a purring trill.
Size of Egg:
31.2—38.3
× 22.4—25.8 mm.

120

Ruff
Philomachus pugnax

Scolopacidae

The ruff is found mainly in the tundras of Europe and Asia, and northern North America. In Europe, however, it also breeds along the coasts of Poland, Germany, Holland, Belgium as well as France and Scotland. During the spring and autumn migration it is encountered in large numbers throughout Europe on the seashore as well as on the shores of lakes, ponds and rivers. The wintering grounds are located in southern and eastern Africa, though some birds pass the winter on the coast of southern and western Europe. The ruff returns to its nesting grounds in large flocks in April, and sometimes as late as May. It likes to nest in wet meadows, moors and marshland, also on the seashore. Courtship begins on the return flight and often observers in central Europe may witness the fascinating display where the males engage in great fights, chopping with their beaks, expanding their magnificent collars or 'ruffs', hopping about, charging, fending off opponents, etc., all of which is only a symbolic show. An interesting feature of the male's striking nuptial plumage is that no two birds are alike in colour. Outside the breeding season the plumage of both sexes is the same. The nest, a shallow hollow lined only sparingly with vegetation, is prepared by the female alone. In May or June she usually lays four eggs which she incubates by herself for twenty to twenty-one days; she likewise rears the young alone. When they are able to fly the birds form flocks that roam the countryside seeking food near water. The diet consists of various invertebrates as well as insects, worms, molluscs and crustaceans, but the birds also eat seeds and small berries.

Length:
Male — 29 cm,
female — 23 cm.
Marked sexual
dimorphism.
Voice:
Muttering sounds
when courting.
Size of Egg:
38.9—48.6
× 28.0—32.8 mm.

122

Red-necked Phalarope — Northern Phalarope

Phalaropus lobatus

Phalaropodidae

The red-necked phalarope breeds in Iceland, northern and western Scandinavia, northern Finland, on the islands off Scotland, in northern Russia and also arctic North America. European populations migrate along the European seacoast but may by seen also on inland waters. Their wintering grounds are the coast of Africa, southern Asia and the Aral Sea. Eastern populations fly as far as Australia and North American populations to South America. Outside the breeding season both the male and female are coloured a drab grey. The red-necked phalarope nests in small groups in marshes, on the shores of lakes and rivers as well as on the seashore. The female selects the site for the nest, which is a hollow in the ground lined with dry grass, leaves and small twigs of the dwarf willow. It is usually well concealed in a grass tussock. The female generally lays four eggs but then leaves the duties of incubating to the male, who also tends the young by himself. The young hatch after twenty to twenty-one days and leave the nest as soon as they are dry. For the first few days they conceal themselves in the vegetation but after about a week they go out on the water. When the young are grown the birds spend most of their time on water, swimming buoyantly on the waves and swinging their heads from left to right as they pick food from the surface with their bills. Every now and then they fly up in the air and settle back on the water again. The diet consists mainly of aquatic insects and their larvae, also flies, molluscs and crustaceans.

Length:
16.5 cm.
The female is more brightly coloured than the male.
Voice:
Short scratchy notes such as 'whit' or 'prip'.
Size of Egg:
26.7 — 34.5
× 19.6 — 22.2 mm.

Avocet

Recurvirostra avosetta

The avocet is found mainly on the coasts of Germany, Denmark and Holland, also southeast England, southern Spain, the Rhône delta and by the Black and Caspian Seas, though it may also be encountered on the salt lakes of southeastern Europe. It prefers marshy localities, sandy shores and islands with bare, open spaces. Some birds are migrant, flying for the winter to South Africa and southern Asia, but many individuals remain on the coasts of southwestern and southeastern Europe. The avocet leaves its breeding grounds between the end of August and the beginning of November, returning again in March to early May. It usually congregates in flocks and likewise during the breeding season it often nests in large colonies. The nest is sited near water in muddy or sandy spots, on grassy areas or in very low vegetation. The nest is a simple scrape sparsely lined with dry grass and small twigs. Between the end of April and June, sometimes even as late as July, the female lays four eggs which both partners incubate for twenty-four to twenty-five days. The young abandon the nest shortly after they have dried out. The avocet obtains its food mainly in shallows where it stamps with its feet on the mud bottom thus stirring up countless small crustaceans and insects which it then captures with rapid sweeping movements of its beak. It also eats small molluscs and sometimes nibbles green vegetable matter, very occasionally also seeds.

Its closest American relative is the American avocet *(Recurvirostra americana)*.

Length:
43 cm.
The male and female have like plumage.
Voice:
A high-pitched flute-like 'kleep' or 'kloo-it'.
Size of Egg:
43.0 — 56.3
× 31.2 — 40.8 mm.

Black-winged Stilt — Black-necked Stilt

Himantopus himantopus

Recurvirostridae

The black-winged stilt is widely distributed in Africa, America, southern Asia, Australia and Europe. In Europe it breeds regularly in Spain, Portugal, southern France and the whole of south-eastern Europe. Very occasionally it breeds also in central Europe and Holland. It inhabits lagoons, seashores, river deltas, large marshes, and the shores of lakes and rivers. It is fond of shallow salt lakes and also the steppes. European birds are migrant and winter in Africa and southern Asia. During migration the black-winged stilt occurs also in Great Britain and Denmark. It generally returns to its breeding grounds in April. It nests in colonies, often together with other species of birds. The nest is a mere scrape near water, lined sparingly with vegetation. Often it is flooded by rising water, in which case the birds build a new nest. In April or May the female usually lays four eggs which she and the male take turns incubating for twenty-five to twenty-six days. The adult birds guard the nest zealously and when danger threatens fly above it in large arcs, uttering loud cries. The newly-hatched young scatter in the neighbourhood of the nest shortly after they are dry. The diet consists of water boatmen and other aquatic insects, also small aquatic molluscs, crustaceans and worms. Occasionally the birds nibble the green parts of plants.

Length:
38 cm.
The male has a dark-coloured crown.
Voice:
A sharp loud cry that sounds like 'kyip, kyip, kyip'.
Size of Egg:
38.8 — 48.2
× 28.0 — 33.5 mm.

Great Skua — Skua
Stercorarius skua

Stercorariidae

The European breeding grounds of the great skua include Iceland, the Faroes, Shetlands, Orkneys and northern Scotland. Interestingly enough, it also breeds on the opposite side of the world from the Antarctic coast to Tierra del Fuego. During the breeding season the great skua is found in marshes near the coast, the nest being located on the ground. The great skua nests in colonies as well as singly. In May or June the female usually lays two eggs which she and her partner incubate for twenty-eight to thirty days. If the clutch is lost she lays again. The young remain in the nest for six to seven weeks, where they are fed by the parents. When they are grown the birds roam the open seas of the eastern Atlantic, often flying as far as the coast of Spain; vagrants may by encountered inland only in rare instances. The great skua feeds on anything it can get hold of, from worms and crustaceans to fish, birds and small mammals. It is particularly fond of the eggs of other birds. It also harasses gulls and terns until they drop or regurgitate their prey, which the great skua quickly picks out of the air and swallows. If nothing else is available it will even gather carcases cast up by the sea. The great skua is a courageous bird and at the nesting site will often chase a falcon and even attacks man. Nowhere throughout its range is it particularly abundant.

Length:
58 cm.
The male and female have like plumage.
Voice:
A low-pitched 'uk-uk-uk', when attacking, 'tuk-tuk'.
Size of Egg:
62.0 — 78.5
× 44.5 — 53.2 mm.

Arctic Skua — Parasitic Jaeger

Stercorarius parasiticus

Stercorariidae

The arctic skua is widespread in the arctic regions of Europe, Asia and North America. In Europe it breeds on the coasts of Scotland, Iceland, western and northern Scandinavia, Finland and northern Russia. Outside the breeding season it keeps to the open seas or coastal waters. When migrating, European populations fly along the coast to western Africa, though single individuals often occur as vagrants inland, rarely, however, in central Europe. During migration arctic skuas often occur in large aggregations. They return to their breeding grounds in April or early May. The arctic skua nests in colonies in the tundra and in marshes. The nests, spaced several tens of metres apart, are shallow depressions in grass without any lining as a rule. The female generally lays two eggs which she begins incubating as soon as the first is laid; the male relieves her at regular intervals. The young hatch after twenty-five to twenty-eight days and are fed by the parents. They are able to fly at the age of thirty-two days, when the birds set out together for their wintering grounds. The arctic skua feeds on small fish, invertebrates, small birds and mammals and is fond of stealing the eggs of other birds. It is likewise fond of chasing gulls, terns and guillemots and robbing them of their prey. Besides this it also eats animal remains cast up by the sea and occasionally even berries.

Length:
66 cm.
The male and female show marked variation in plumage coloration, ranging from a distinct light phase to a distinct dark phase.
Voice:
A guttural 'eee-air'.
Size of Egg:
49.0 — 63.1 × 37.2 — 44.3 mm.

Great Black-backed Gull

Larus marinus

Laridae

The great black-backed gull is widespread in Iceland, on the coasts of Scandinavia and Finland, in Ireland and on the west coasts of England and Scotland. Occasionally it nests on the west coast of France and in Denmark. It also nests in Greenland and on the eastern coast of northern North America. It is locally resident but in winter many individuals roam the European coasts westward from Poland and southward as far as Spain. It is rarely encountered inland. It nests in colonies, often together with the lesser black-backed gull, as well as singly. It inhabits rocky coasts and islands as well as marshes and lake islands. The nest is built by both partners, usually on a rock ledge, less often on the ground. It is made of twigs, grass, seaweeds and other vegetable matter and is lined with feathers. In May or June, very occasionally also in late April, the female lays two or three eggs which she and her partner take turns incubating for twenty-six to twenty-eight days. The newly-hatched nestlings weigh about eighty grams. They soon leave the nest and scatter in the neighbourhood, concealing themselves in the vegetation. The adult birds bring them food for almost fifty days. The flight feathers grow in when the nestlings are forty-five days old but they do not fly well until the age of two months. The diet consists of fish, small birds and their eggs, crustaceans, molluscs, and animal remains.

Length:
74 cm.
The male and female have like plumage.
Voice:
Usually a low-pitched and harsh 'owk'.
Size of Egg:
67.5 — 87.0
× 49.0 — 57.6 mm.

Lesser Black-backed Gull

Larus fuscus

Laridae

The lesser black-backed gull has a comparatively small range. It inhabits Scandinavia, Finland, Iceland, the British Isles and Ireland, Denmark, the coasts of Germany and western France, and also breeds in northern Siberia. It is mostly a migrant; only in England and Ireland is it generally resident.

It winters on the coasts of western and southern Europe and North Africa, some birds as far away as western Africa. It flies along rivers and thus may be encountered at this time also in central Europe. Young, non-breeding birds, however, roam far and wide even during the nesting period. April is when the lesser black-backed gull returns to its breeding grounds, seeking out islands or rocky coasts, river deltas and bodies of freshwater near the sea. It nests in colonies, being partial to grassy sites. The nest is made of sticks, seaweed and other vegetable matter and lined with fine plant remnants, feathers and the like. The clutch usually consists of three eggs, which are laid in May or June. They are incubated by both partners for a period of twenty-six to twenty-seven days. The young abandon the nest soon after hatching, though they sometimes remain there several days if they are not disturbed. They are fed by both parents, mostly small fish. When they have fledged, groups of young and adult birds roam the countryside together. The lesser black-backed gull feeds mostly on fish, especially herring, but it also catches small mammals, as well as small birds.

Its nearest American relative is the herring gull (*Larus argentatus*).

Length:
53 cm.
The male and female have like plumage.
Voice:
A deep, loud cry that sounds like 'goh-goh-goh'.
Size of Egg:
57.5 — 77.1 × 43.0 — 52.1 mm.

Herring Gull

Larus argentatus

Laridae

The herring gull is widespread in Europe, Asia, North America and Africa. In Europe it breeds practically along all the coasts from the Baltic and North Seas, down the Atlantic to the Mediterranean, and along the Black and Caspian Sea coasts. It is a migrant as well as partial migrant. Outside the breeding season it occurs in large flocks in harbours where it scavenges for fish remnants from the fishing boats. It nests in colonies on islands and cliffs as well as in reed beds. Colonies sometimes number several thousand pairs. On the Bulgarian coast it even nests on the roofs of houses. The nest is made of sticks and bits of vegetation and is located in reed beds on a pile of bent, flattened reeds. In May or June the female usually lays three eggs. If the clutch is lost, she lays a new lot of eggs. Both partners incubate for twenty-six to twenty-eight days. The young birds scatter about the neighbourhood of the nest the day after hatching, concealing themselves in clumps of grass and amidst the reeds. They are fed by the adult birds even when they are able to fly, which is at the age of forty to forty-two days. The herring gull eats various remnants cast up by the sea, refuse, as well as the eggs of birds and their young. In recent years it has been accorded rigid protection in many places but has multiplied so abundantly that it has caused great damage to the nests of other birds, particularly ducks and terns, and thus measures have had to be taken to regulate its numbers.

Length:
56 cm.
The male and female have like plumage.
Voice:
A ringing 'kyow', also
'gah-gah-gah'.
Size of Egg:
58.0 — 82.7
× 44.1 — 54.8 mm.

Common Gull — Mew Gull

Larus canus

Laridae

The common gull breeds on the shores of Scandinavia, Finland, Russia, Great Britain, Ireland, Denmark, Germany, Poland and very occasionally also the shores of Holland, Belgium and France. Outside the breeding season it may be seen throughout practically the whole of Europe, mostly, however, along the coasts. It often also occurs as a vagrant inland in central Europe. Birds arrive at their nesting grounds in March or early April already paired. They nest in colonies. The nest is placed on rock ledges, on islands in grass or in reeds. It is constructed mainly by the female, while the male usually keeps his distance, now and then bringing a piece of building material to his mate. In colonies the nests are generally spaced several metres apart. The clutch, as a rule, consists of three eggs, which the two partners take turns incubating at intervals of two to three hours. The young hatch after twenty-five to twenty-six days and leave the nest at the age of one or two days, but remain in the vicinity. They are tended by both parents who bring them food — insects and small fish the first four days, which the young take from their beaks. When they are twenty days old the young gulls forage for food themselves, gathering insects and their larvae, worms and molluscs, but also continue to be fed by the parents. Not till the age of thirty-five days are they fully independent. The favourite fish of this gull are cod and herring.

Length:
40 cm.
The male and female have like plumage.
Voice:
A high-pitched cry that sounds like 'gah-gah-gah'.
Size of Egg:
50.0 — 67.2
× 35.9 — 45.4 mm.

Little Gull

Larus minutus

Laridae

The little gull is widely distributed from the Baltic seacoast of Finland and southern Sweden east through Poland and Russia to eastern Siberia. It is also found in North America. Very occasionally it breeds also along the coast of Denmark and the northern coast of the Black Sea. It is found mostly along the seashore and in river deltas, also, however, on inland lakes. A large number of these birds winter in the Mediterranean, many also in western Europe and the Baltic Sea. During migration the little gull may be seen regularly even in the heart of central Europe. It nests in colonies numbering two to fifty pairs, often together with terns and other gulls, usually in marshes. The nest, built by both partners, is placed on a mound of reeds or on the ground and is constructed of dry as well as green plant parts. It generally measures fifty centimetres across, the nesting hollow about ten centimetres across, and is about twenty centimetres high. At the end of May or in June, very occasionally even in July, the female lays two to three eggs which she and her partner take turns incubating for twenty to twenty-one days. The young generally leave the nest the very first day and conceal themselves in the surrounding vegetation where the parents bring them food. They begin to fly at the age of twenty-five days. The little gull captures insects in the air or on the water: it also eats molluscs, crustaceans, worms and occasionally even small fish.

Length:
28 cm.
The male and female have like plumage.
Voice:
Not too loud 'kek-kek-kek' or a whistling 'kay-ee'.
Size of Egg:
37.0 — 45.8 × 27.3 — 32.0 mm.

Kittiwake —
Black-legged Kittiwake

Rissa tridactyla

The kittiwake is found in Europe along the coasts of Norway, Iceland, the British Isles, Ireland and the Murmansk region. Very occasionally it nests also in Heligoland and on the coast of Brittany. Outside the breeding season European birds stay out on the open sea, mostly in the middle Atlantic. Only on rare occasions do young birds stray inland. The kittiwake breeds in large colonies on the narrow rock ledges of steep cliffs but sometimes it sites its nest on the ledges of tall buildings in cities, particularly Norwegian ports. The nest, a sturdy structure with a deep hollow, is built by both partners of lichens, moss, seaweeds and other plant matter held together with clay or mud. The eggs, only two as a rule, are laid in May or June, occasionally in July, and both partners take turns incubating them for twenty-one to twenty-four days. The young, unlike those of other gulls, remain in the nest for thirty-three to thirty-seven days until they are able to fly, being fed by the parents the whole time. When they have fledged the entire colony leaves the nesting site for the open sea. The diet consists mostly of marine animals, particularly fish, crustaceans and molluscs, but the kittiwake also eats plant food. It obtains its food in flight from the water's surface.

Length:
40 cm.
The male and female have like plumage.
Voice:
In the nesting grounds its call sounds like 'kitti-wack' or 'kaka-week'.
Size of Egg:
47.1 — 62.5
× 35.3 — 44.5 mm.

Caspian Tern
Hydroprogne caspia

Laridae

The Caspian tern has a disrupted range but is found practically throughout the world. In Europe it breeds on the eastern coast of Sweden, Finland, and the northern shores of the Caspian and Black Seas. Occasionally it nests also on the northern coasts of West Germany and in Sardinia. It is a bird of the seashore. After the breeding season it flies to its winter quarters along the shores of tropical regions. Only rarely does it stray inland into central Europe. April/May is when it returns to its breeding grounds. The Caspian tern nests in colonies, often large ones, generally on sandy beaches or small islands. The nesting hollow is only sparingly lined with plant matter. In May or June the female lays two eggs as a rule; these are incubated by both partners for twenty to twenty-two days. Shortly after they have hatched the young scatter throughout the neighbourhood, concealing themselves in the vegetation where the adult birds bring them food. At the age of thirty to thirty-five days they are able to fly and fend for themselves. The Caspian tern feeds mainly on fish, mostly herring, but also eats various invertebrates and occasionally also small birds and their eggs. When it seeks fish it flies above the water, hovering in one spot every once in a while and then plummeting downward to the water.

Length:
53 cm.
The male and female have like plumage.
Voice:
A very deep 'kaah' or 'kraa-uh'.
Size of Egg:
55.0 — 72.3
× 40.5 — 46.5 mm.

Arctic Tern
Sterna paradisaea

The arctic tern is widespread in the northern regions of the Old and New World. In Europe it breeds in Iceland, Scandinavia, on the coasts of Poland, Germany, Denmark, Holland, the British Isles, Ireland, Brittany and northern Russia. It is found chiefly on seashores and rocky islands, also on inland lakes in Iceland and Scandinavia. When migrating it flies along the coast as far as the tip of South Africa, whence many individuals continue on to the shores of the Antarctic. The birds return to their breeding grounds in April or early May. The nest is usually just a shallow scrape without any lining; only sometimes is it lined with small shell fragments and the like. In May or June the female usually lays two, very occasionally only one or three eggs, which she and her partner take turns incubating. The young hatch after twenty to twenty-two days and soon abandon the nest to scatter in the neighbourhood. They continue to be fed by their parents even when they are already capable of flight, which is usually at the age of four weeks. The arctic tern obtains its food in flight from the water, only very occasionally catching insects also on the ground. It also eats small fish, molluscs, worms and crustaceans. The arctic tern has many enemies, especially amongst larger gulls, skuas, raptorial birds and predators. In colonies its eggs and young suffer marked losses — usually only about sixteen per cent of the offspring reach maturity.

Length:
38 cm.
The male and female have like plumage.
Voice:
A short call that sounds like 'kee-kee' or 'kria'.
Size of Egg:
35.3 — 47.3
× 26.2 — 33.4 mm.

Roseate Tern

Sterna dougallii

The roseate tern has a wide range of distribution embracing the Atlantic coast of North America, the coast of Central America, the Antilles, the African coast and southeast Asia. In Europe it breeds mainly on the coasts of the British Isles and Ireland. At one time it also nested in the south of France and on the North Friesian Islands, but occurs there no more. European birds winter on the islands of the Atlantic and on the western coast of Africa. When migrating they occur on occasion also on the coast of West Germany and Holland. The roseate tern has a discontinuous distribution and occurs only along the seashore. It nests in large colonies on sandy or rocky peninsulas and islands, often together with other terns. The eggs, usually two, very occasionally three, are laid in a shallow, unlined depression or merely on the bare, hard ground. In Europe they are generally laid in June and are incubated by both partners for twenty-one days. Both likewise share the duties of feeding their offspring for over a month. After the young are grown the birds roam the seacoasts in large flocks, setting out for their winter quarters at the end of July or in August. The diet consists chiefly of small fish but the roseate tern also hunts water insects and their larvae as well as molluscs, crustaceans and worms. The roseate tern has many enemies, particularly amongst the larger gulls, which steal its eggs and young from the nest.

Length:
38 cm.
The male and female have like plumage.
Voice:
A long 'aaak', soft 'chu-ick', also 'kekekekek'.
Size of Egg:
38.0 — 47.0
× 30.0 — 32.0 mm.

Little Tern — Least Tern

Sterna albifrons

Laridae

The little tern is the smallest of the European terns and is found in the temperate zone of nearly all the continents. In Europe it breeds along practically the entire Atlantic coast and sometimes also inland; it is absent, however, in Iceland, Scandinavia and the northern parts of Europe. It inhabits sandy and gravelly locations as well as marshy areas bordering lakes and rivers. A migratory bird, it leaves its breeding grounds by the end of July for its winter quarters along the coasts of the Indian Ocean, returning again in late April or the beginning of May. It nests in small colonies, the nests being spaced quite far apart. Often it joins colonies of Kentish plovers. The nest is a shallow depression in the ground sparingly lined with small stones or shells. In the second half of May and in June the female usually lays two eggs which show marked variation in colouring. They are incubated mostly by the female, though the male relieves her now and then. The young hatch after twenty-one to twenty-two days and for the first few days of their life are kept warm by the mother while the male brings them food. Later they are fed by both parents. The diet consists of small fish, to a lesser extent also invertebrates. The little tern catches insects both on the water and on the ground. It catches fish by plunging after them from the air.

Length:
20 cm.
The male and female nave like plumage.
Voice:
A high-pitched 'kree-ik' or harsh 'kitt'.
Size of Egg:
29.5 — 37.0 × 20.8 — 26.0 mm.

Sandwich Tern — Cabot's Tern

Sterna sandvicensis

Laridae

The sandwich tern is widespread in Europe, by the Caspian Sea, as well as in Tunisia and North America, but its distribution is discontinuous and circumscribed. Regular European breeding grounds include southern Sweden, Denmark, Germany, Holland, Brittany, the British Isles, Spain and the shores of the Black Sea. In the autumn it departs for Africa, often flying as far as South Africa and the Persian Gulf. Only very occasionally does it stray inland. The sandwich tern forms dense colonies, sometimes numbering as many as a thousand pairs. It nests only on the seashore and on islands, being partial to locations covered partly with grass. The nests, shallow depressions only sparingly lined with varied plant material, are often spaced only ten to fifteen centimetres apart. In May or early June the female usually lays two eggs which she and her mate incubate for twenty-one to twenty-four days. The young remain in the nest for six to seven days, sometimes even a bit longer, and then scatter in the neighbourhood. At the age of fifteen to twenty days the young birds join to form flocks and at the age of thirty-five days they are already able to fly. The sandwich tern feeds chiefly on fish, mainly herring, mackerel, etc. It hunts its prey by plunging headlong into the water from the air. Besides fish it also eats molluscs, crustaceans, worms and sometimes even small birds. On the rare occasion it will even eat insects.

Length:
40 cm.
The male and female have like plumage.
Voice:
A harsh cry that sounds like 'kirrik'.
Size of Egg:
44.0 — 59.4 × 33.3 — 43.2 mm.

Razorbill
Alca torda

The razorbill is found on the seacoasts of practically all of Scandinavia, the Murmansk region, Ireland, the British Isles, Iceland and Heligoland, its range extending to the coast of Brittany. It also occurs in Greenland and in northern North America. It is definitely a bird of the open seas, roaming the expanses of the Atlantic outside the breeding season. The razorbill is a gregarious bird and nests in large colonies on rock cliffs on islands and on the coast, building no nest but laying its single egg on a rock ledge, under a boulder or in a rock crevice, or sometimes even in the abandoned nest of a kittiwake. The egg, laid between mid-May and June, is incubated by both parents usually for thirty-two to thirty-six days. Both likewise share the duties of rearing and feeding their offspring. When the young bird is about seventeen to twenty-one days old it leaves its 'nest' and leaps into the water, sometimes hitting the rocks as it falls for it is still not very adept at flying. However, in the water it is immediately able to swim and dive. The diet consists chiefly of small fish in search of which the birds sometimes fly as far as twenty kilometres from the nest during the breeding season. In the water the razorbill is able to hold several fish in its beak at one time. It also hunts crustaceans, molluscs and marine worms. It is an excellent diver.

Length:
40 cm.
The male and female have like plumage.
Voice:
Long, whistling notes.
Size of Egg:
63.0 — 83.6
× 42.0 — 52.4 mm.

Guillemot — Common Murre

Uria aalge

Alcidae

The northern and western coasts of Scandinavia, the Murmansk region, Iceland, the British Isles, sometimes also Brittany, Portugal, Spain and some islands in the North and Baltic Seas are the European breeding grounds of the guillemot. Some young as well as adult birds stay the winter near the nesting site but most roam the open seas of the Atlantic. The guillemot occurs very occasionally as a visitor inland. It arrives at its breeding grounds in December or January, in the extreme northern parts of its range not till March. It nests in colonies on cliffs. In the British Isles and the Baltic Sea area the birds begin to lay eggs in mid-May. The single egg is laid directly on the hard rock, sometimes, however, the female places a small stone or bit of grass under the egg and may even deposit it in a kittiwake's nest. Eggs vary considerably in colour. The parents take turns incubating for thirty to thirty-six days and then feed their offspring, which are covered with a thick coat of down, two to three times a day, a diet mainly of fish. At the age of twenty to twenty-five days the young bird leaves the nest though as yet unable to fly; it merely spreads its wings and drops down onto the water. The adult birds continue to feed it a while longer on the water. The diet consists of small fish but the guillemot also hunts crustaceans, marine worms and molluscs.

Length:
43 cm.
The male and female have like plumage.
Voice:
A long 'arrr' or 'arra'.
Size of Egg:
74.0 — 93.0
× 46.0 — 55.0 mm.

Brünnich's Guillemot — Thick-billed Murre

Uria lomvia

Alcidae

The northernmost arctic regions of Asia, North America, Greenland and Europe are the home of Brünnich's guillemot. In Europe it breeds only in Iceland and on the Murmansk coast. In winter it may be seen along the northern coast of Norway and round Iceland, occasionally as far as the north of France and the Baltic Sea. Only rarely does it stray inland. It arrives at its breeding grounds in late March or early April, keeping to the water at first and then settling on the steep cliffs. It nests in large colonies on rock ledges, laying the single egg on the bare rock. The young bird is covered with a thick coat of down resembling the fur of mammals. The adult birds bring food to their offspring as often as three times daily, flying for it as far as fifteen kilometres from the nesting site. At the age of eighteen to twenty-five days the young bird abandons the nest. Though yet unable to fly it rapidly flutters its wings as it drops towards the water thus lessening the impact of the fall. Whole flocks of young birds then swim on the sea uttering loud cries and calling to the adult birds. The parents fly after their offspring and continue to feed them at sea. Brünnich's guillemot hunts in flocks of twenty to two hundred birds; its chief prey are fish five to fifteen centimetres long but it also eats crustaceans and molluscs. On land it walks upright and slowly. In water it swims buoyantly and dives expertly, but not to great depths.

Length:
39 to 48 cm.
The male and female have like plumage.
Voice:
A whistling 'arr'.
Size of Egg:
69.0 — 99.0
× 41.0 — 59.0 mm.

Black Guillemot

Cepphus grylle

Alcidae

The black guillemot is widely distributed in Europe and in the northern parts of Asia and North America. Its European breeding grounds are the coasts of Scandinavia, Finland, the Murmansk region, Iceland, Scotland, Ireland and Denmark. It is mostly resident but in winter flocks may be seen along the coasts of Germany. Outside the breeding season it stays close inshore at sea. The black guillemot seeks a suitable nesting site one to two weeks before laying its eggs when the ice and snow have thawed. It nests singly or in small groups numbering several tens of paired birds; only rarely do the colonies number several hundred pairs. The nest is usually located in a rock crevice, under a rock ledge, sometimes even in a vertical burrow. Between mid-May and mid-June the female usually lays two eggs on the bare rock, sometimes placing several small stones underneath. Both partners take turns incubating the eggs which at this time register a temperature of 35°—37°C, though on the side resting on the ground the temperature is only 16°—19°C. The young hatch after twenty-seven to thirty days. Lying on their bellies they are fed by the parents from the second day on; the adult birds generally bring them small fish three to five times daily. At the age of thirty-five to thirty-seven days the young leave the nest, usually at night, and go out on the sea. The mainstay of the diet is small fish, other food being insects, molluscs and crustaceans. The black guillemot swims and dives well.

Length:
32 to 38 cm.
The male and female have like plumage.
Voice:
Whistling notes and twittering trills.
Size of Egg:
57.0—65.0
× 38.0—44.0 mm.

Puffin — Common Puffin
Fratercula arctica

The puffin is at home on the coasts and islands of the northern and middle Atlantic. In Europe it nests on the coasts of the Murmansk region, Norway, southwest Sweden, Great Britain, Ireland, Iceland and Brittany. It is a bird of the open seas and outside the breeding season keeps to the middle Atlantic waters. Before the nesting period it arrives on the coasts in large flocks seeking out soft grassy slopes in which it can dig its burrows more easily. However, it is also content with rocky locations where it can nest in cavities, crevices or rabbit holes. As a rule, with the aid of both feet and beak, it digs its own burrows; these measure one to two metres in length and have one or more nesting chambers and several corridors. The chambers are lined with dry grass, feathers or marine plants brought from the sea. The puffin nests in large colonies sometimes numbering more than a hundred thousand birds. The single egg, which is very large and often weighs more than one tenth the body weight of the female, is usually laid in May and incubated by both partners for forty to forty-two days. The puffin feeds mainly on fish, but also eats molluscs and crustaceans. The adult birds often carry several fish in the beak at one time, sometimes as many as twelve. They obtain their food underwater, where they swim with the aid of both feet and wings.

Length:
28 to 37 cm.
The male and female have like plumage.
Voice:
Heard only occasionally, on the breeding grounds the call consists of notes that sound like 'ow' or 'arr'.
Size of Egg:
58.0 — 68.0
× 39.0 — 49.0 mm.

Snowy Owl
Nyctea scandiaca

The snowy owl is a bird of the arctic tundras of Europe, Asia, North America and Greenland. In Europe it breeds in Iceland and on the coasts of Norway and the Murmansk region. Outside the breeding season it occurs in large numbers on sea and lake shores. Very occasionally it strays as far as central and western Europe. It is partial to open country and avoids woodlands. During its winter wanderings it perches on ice-floes or rocks from which it has a good view of the surrounding country. The nesting territory measures about one square kilometre and when food is scarce as much as two square kilometres. The nest is built on the ground on a slight rise, on a rock ledge, and is richly lined with feathers. The female usually lays four to six eggs, in years when food is plentiful as many as fifteen. They are incubated by the female alone for thirty-two to thirty-four days during which time the male brings her food. When they hatch the young are covered with a thick layer of down. The first few days the female tears the prey into pieces before feeding it to her offspring. The youngsters usually remain in the nest fifty-seven to sixty-one days, at which time they are ready to fly. The snowy owl flies near the ground with fluttering wingbeats on the lookout for lemmings, which are the mainstay of its diet. In one year a single owl devours 600 to 1,600 of these creatures, i.e. a total weight of 55 to 130 kilograms. Two lemmings are the average daily fare of a single nestling. In years when the lemming population is small the snowy owl often does not nest at all; it then hunts ducks, geese, ptarmigan, alcids, gulls, as well as squirrels and stoats for food.

Length:
54 to 66 cm.
The male is white, the female spotted.
Voice:
A loud repeated 'krow-ow' or a repeated 'rick'.
Size of Egg:
50.5 — 70.2
× 40.0 — 49.3 mm.

RARE VISITORS TO EUROPEAN COASTS

Europe's seacoasts, which extend across several parallels and meridians, are naturally host to a wide variety of birds. Certain birds breed in the north, others round the Mediterranean. Sometimes birds do not remain within the boundaries of their usual range and may be encountered as visitors in far distant places. However, we shall consider as visitors to Europe's shores only those species that do not breed in Europe and do not occur there regularly in great numbers but only as occasional vagrants.

In the winter months on the shores of Iceland, France, England and Spain, one may come across Sabine's gull *(Larus sabini)*, which breeds in the arctic regions, in Alaska, arctic Canada and arctic Siberia, often in the company of the arctic tern. Where it passes the winter is not established as yet. It visits Europe's coasts in small groups.

An even rarer visitor to these shores is the graceful Ross's gull *(Rhodostethia rosea)*. It is rare even in its native habitat in northern Siberia, where it breeds in the arctic tundras in small colonies of two to twenty pairs. In winter it roams in small flocks along the boundaries of the arctic regions of Asia and North America and only the occasional individual occurs on the coast of western Europe.

In Scotland and Ireland, in winter, one may encounter the Iceland gull *(Larus glaucoides)*, which breeds on the coast of Greenland and very occasionally off the coast of Iceland, where, however, it regularly spends the winter.

Europe's extreme northern coast is on rare occasions the winter home of the ivory gull *(Pagophila eburnea)* which has snow-white plumage. This pretty gull breeds in the extreme northern arctic on Greenland's northern coast, in the Parry Islands, and on the northern shores of Baffin Island, as well as in Spitsbergen, Franz Josef Land, the northern part of

Novaya Zemlya and on the Novosibirsk Islands. Very occasionally it occurs in winter on the coast of Iceland, in the Faroes, northern Scandinavia, the Orkneys and also the Shetlands.

The year 1968 was probably the first time Europe was visited by the ring-billed gull *(Larus delawarensis)*, which was encountered near Brunswick. This gull breeds in the north-western United States and in Canada. Bonaparte's gull *(Larus philadelphia)* likewise strays from North America to western Europe as an occasional visitor. A fairly frequent visitor to Europe is the pomarine skua *(Stercorarius pomarinus)* which breeds in northern Asia and North America.

A very rare visitor from the southern seas, encountered now and then on Europe's western shores, is the black-browed albatross *(Diomedea melanophris)*, which breeds in the Falklands, Kerguelen, the islands off Auckland, the southern part of Georgia and the islands of the southernmost seas. It is remarkable that this bird flies thousands of kilometres northward across the equator as far as Scotland and Iceland where it has generally been encountered in colonies of gannets. Also met with very occasionally in Europe is the wandering albatross *(Diomedea exulans)*.

Wilson's petrel *(Oceanites oceanicus)* is another visitor from the Antarctic. It nests from December till February in the Falklands, the southern parts of Georgia and in the Orkneys. After the young have fledged it sets out on its northward journey, flying as far as Labrador and the British Isles. Recently it has also been encountered in Hamburg.

Chief of the rare waterfowl visitors is the lovely king eider *(Somateria spectabilis)*, which breeds along the arctic coasts of the U.S.S.R., North America and Greenland. Individual birds may be encountered in winter on the coast of Norway, Iceland and Scotland. A very rare visitor to the coast of Norway is the spectacled eider *(Somateria fischeri)* of northern Siberia and Alaska.

A regular visitor to Norway's northern coast is Steller's eider *(Polysticta stelleri)*, which likewise breeds in the coastal regions of Siberia and Alaska. Occasionally it may also be encountered on the coasts of England, Ireland, France, Denmark and Germany. Barrow's goldeneye *(Bucephala albeola)* of North America, which winters regularly in the southern United States, sometimes strays as far as Great Britain, flying to Europe across the Atlantic. Another visitor from arctic North America is the snow goose *(Chen hyperborea)*.

The red-breasted goose *(Branta ruficollis)* is a rare visitor to France, Great Britain and Iceland. However, this nicely coloured goose has already been encountered in nearly all European countries. Its nesting grounds are to be found in the arctic tundra of northern Siberia and it winters regularly on the Caspian Sea coast. It strays to Europe in small flocks.

The upland sandpiper *(Bartramia longicauda),* which winters in South America as a rule, sometimes journeys from North America all the way to the British Isles, Denmark, West Germany and Italy.

The lesser golden plover *(Pluvialis dominica)* of arctic Siberia and North America may on rare occasions be encountered in the British Isles, Heligoland, Norway, Holland, Italy and Spain. An extremely rare visitor is the buff-breasted sandpiper *(Tryngites subruficollis),* which breeds in northern Siberia and Alaska and winters regularly in southeastern Asia and along the coast of Australia.

These, of course, are not the only birds that are encountered on Europe's shores. Others, too, may stray here from their far-off homes.

PROTECTION OF SEA
AND COASTAL BIRDS

Sea birds have been protected in some places since days of old. Mention has already been made of how the Inca rulers long ago forbade access to the bird islands off the coast of Peru. There the birds were not disturbed or hunted in the past, nor are they today.

In former days, however, protection of sea birds was the exception rather than the rule and man is even responsible for the extinction of some species. One example is the great auk *(Pinguinus impennis)*. We do not know the range of its original breeding grounds, but in the 18th and 19th century it still nested in fair abundance in Iceland, on the coasts of Ireland, Scotland and Newfoundland, in the Hebrides and Faroes, on the coasts of Denmark, southern Sweden, Norway and Greenland and on the eastern coast of North America. In the 18th century its eggs were still being gathered in large numbers. However, not only did hunters take the eggs, they also killed adult birds for their feathers, meat and fat, which they sold. Catching a great auk was very easy for it was a flightless bird and all the hunters had to do was block its access to the sea. By the beginning of the 19th century the great auk was already a rare bird. The last great auk population died in 1830 when a volcano erupted off the coast of Iceland. The last existing pair of these birds was killed by hunters on the island of Eldey near Iceland on 3 June 1844. Today this sea bird is quite extinct, and there remain only seventy-four specimens in various museum collections.

The great auk was not the only bird that has become extinct as a species. The same fate was met by the Labrador duck *(Camptorhynchus labradorius)*, which nested in Labrador and on the rocky islands round the Gulf of St. Lawrence and wintered in the area stretching from the coast of Nova Scotia to New Jersey. It was very numerous at one time but none of our generation has ever seen it alive. The history of this duck is very brief. It was first discovered in 1788 by scientists. Thirty years later the land was settled by man and the islands where the birds nested were visited by large numbers of hunters who shot the birds and took the eggs from their nests. The Labrador duck thus disappeared very quickly. The last one was shot in 1875 near Long Island. Today there are only forty-two specimens in museum collections and not one egg has survived.

Several other sea birds have become extinct, including the spectacled cormorant *(Phalacrocorax perspicillatus)*, which at one time nested in large numbers in the Komandorskie Islands, and many other species have survived only thanks to timely protective measures.

In the first half of the twentieth century the number of guillemots *(Uria aalge)* in Labrador, on the coasts of Norway, Sweden, Iceland, Greenland and other places, declined alarmingly. Other alcids, too, were killed for their meat and their eggs, which were gathered in large numbers. In some breeding grounds certain species have disappeared altogether, for example the puffin in Labrador and Heligoland. In the past puffins were killed for their tasty meat, which according to experts was as good as that of the partridge. Even though in many places these birds are now protected, in others they continue to be hunted even to this day. They are caught in flight in nets attached to long poles and the number captured each year in all the breeding grounds equals more than a million birds. Today, the puffin breeds on the coasts of Norway, Iceland, Greenland, Great Britain, the western coast of France and eastern coast of North America. It forms colonies containing several hundreds to thousands of birds. The entire world population is estimated at fifteen million and in view of the fact that many breeding grounds have been proclaimed wildlife reserves there is no threat to the survival of this bird, even though it is hunted in places.

Guillemots and razorbills were also killed in large numbers in the past, but the greatest damage was caused through the gathering of their eggs. It is estimated that until recently some ten million eggs of the guillemot and one million eggs of Brünnich's guillemot were gathered yearly. Hunters captured, and in some places still do, adult guillemots and razorbills in snares. Their meat does not smell of fish and is considered a delicacy by the natives. Their skins are used by Eskimoes for making outer garments.

Fresh sea bird eggs were at one time eaten in great quantity and in many places still are today. In some places it is still permitted to collect eggs, but only those of the first clutch, for in such a case birds will lay a second clutch within fifteen to twenty days. In northerly regions, however, conditions are not as conducive to rearing the young of the second clutch. In addition, eggs may be collected only in such nesting grounds as are not visited by foxes, which destroy not only the eggs but kill young nestlings as well. If provided with full protection a colony of birds has a potential increase of only about ten per cent a year, but if only the second clutch is protected by law then at most the colony retains its status quo unless its numbers are depleted by other circumstances such as natural enemies, bad weather, and the like.

Somewhat better off was the eider. Even though its eggs were gathered in some places it was protected in general. However, this was not primarily for conservationist but for mercenary reasons, the same as the birds of the 'guano' cliffs, because the soft down which the duck plucks from her breast to line the nest is a lucrative item of commerce. Fresh down that has not become soiled is the most valuable. When the down is taken from the nest the duck plucks out further down to replace it, usually after she has begun incubating. This down, however, is of lesser value for it is generally soiled. In order to provide eiders with more opportunities for nesting, 'down farmers' in many places construct hollows of stones or place tree trunks on the shore underneath which eiders are fond of building their nests. The eiders are disturbed by no one here apart from the down collectors and they have therefore no fear of man. Eiders are very plentiful in protected areas. Paired birds build their nests close beside each other thus forming whole colonies. A single nest generally contains about fifteen grams, occasionally as much as thirty-five grams, of eiderdown and one collector can gather about two kilograms of down a day. The greatest supply of eiderdown comes from Iceland, where it was already harvested centuries ago and where, according to records, eiders were protected in some places from as early as 1281. Since 1702 eiders throughout the whole of Iceland have been protected by law and killing just a single bird was punished by a heavy jail sentence. In 1805 Iceland sold 1,072 kilograms of eiderdown and in 1916 4,355 kilograms, which is the equivalent of down from more than 220,000 nests. This number represents practically all the nests of the Iceland population, which is estimated at about half a million.

Eiderdown has also been gathered for almost a thousand years on the coast of Norway. Though the eider is now protected in that country it is still occasionally hunted. There are about 200,000 eiders in Norway, 100,000 in Finland, 80,000 on the coasts of Great Britain, and over 5,000 in Denmark. The total European population numbers about one million birds and the world population is an estimated two million.

Many other waterfowl, notably geese, are far worse off and some species have to be strictly protected not only during the breeding season but also in their wintering grounds. One such is the red-breasted goose *(Branta ruficollis)*, which breeds in the northern parts of central Siberia, flying to northern Azerbaijan for the winter. At present shooting or catching this bird for export is strictly prohibited in Russia for the entire population numbers an estimated 40,000 birds at the most.

The barnacle goose *(Branta leucopsis)* is not much better off as regards numbers. It is found in the northern part of the Atlantic and winters on the coasts of western Europe. From Greenland it also journeys to the eastern coast of North America. The number of all wintering birds is only 30,000 or so.

The brent goose *(Branta bernicla)* breeds in the arctic tundras of Europe, Asia and North America. Its numbers have declined markedly during the past few decades. At the beginning of this century some 350,000 of these birds wintered in Europe, whereas by the 1950s there were only 20,000. The

American populations comprise ninety per cent of all existing brent geese, their estimated number being 175,000.

Other species of geese have also declined markedly in number compared with past years. The white-fronted goose *(Anser albifrons)* of northern Europe, Asia and North America winters in western and southern Europe, Asia Minor, northern India, eastern China, Japan and on the Atlantic coast of North America. Holland is host to 50,000 of these geese in winter, England to some 7,000. The estimated number of white-fronted geese in the whole world is half a million.

Much rarer is the lesser white-fronted goose *(Anser erythropus)*, which has an estimated world population of 100,000. It breeds in the tundras of Europe and Asia and winters in western Europe, Asia Minor, south of the Caspian Sea as well as in northeastern Asia and in the Nile region.

The bean goose *(Anser fabalis)* has likewise become less plentiful in recent years. Its breeding grounds are the arctic regions of Europe and Asia and the coasts of Greenland. In Europe it winters in the western and southern parts. In some places it occurs in greater numbers. In Iceland there are 50,000 of these birds.

Today, probably the most numerous of geese is the snow goose *(Chen hyperborea)*, even though there were far more of these birds at the beginning of the twentieth century than there are now. Doubtlessly one of the reasons for its decline, though not the chief one, was the shooting of these birds during the moulting period when they are unable to fly. The snow goose breeds mainly along the coast in places that are easily accessible. Eskimos killed hundreds and even thousands of these birds during the moulting period besides also taking their eggs. The greater part of the Siberian population wintered in southwestern North America, where birds that breed on Wrangel Island still winter to this day. In the 1840s the wintering grounds were visited by many hunters from Europe and the eastern United States, a hundred geese being killed in one day by a single hunter. Nowadays the snow goose is found in greater numbers in Asia only on Wrangel Island and in its former breeding grounds in Siberia, where it is becoming more plentiful every year. The greatest number of snow geese, however, breeds in arctic Canada, where the population is estimated at 500,000 birds. There are probably only 1 to 1.5 million of these birds in the whole world.

One of the sea birds that has again become more plentiful thanks to conservation measures is the gannet *(Sula bassana)*. Its numbers had been rapidly declining because the eggs, and also the young birds, were being taken from the nest. The feathers lining the nest were also collected. The number of gannets in the nineteenth century was about 330,000 whereas by the end of the century it was a mere 60,000. Most of the birds were killed in the years 1880 to 1910 when fishermen raided the nesting grounds of the gannet — their 'competitor' for the herring catch.

In many places today sea birds are strictly protected in wildlife reserves and their populations are again growing. Ranking among the leading countries in bird protection are Sweden, Norway, Great Britain, Russia, East and West Germany as well as other European maritime countries.

Not everywhere, alas, is the protection of sea birds rigidly enforced. In many breeding grounds the birds' eggs are collected from their nests. In the Seychelles alone some one million terns' eggs are collected yearly. Millions of eggs belonging to gulls, terns and other birds nesting in easily accessible places are collected annually in other colonies as well.

Another threat to sea birds has loomed in recent years: oil. Every year oil tankers are damaged at sea and the oil spills into the water causing the death of thousands upon thousands of sea birds. In some places hundreds of conservationists have come to the aid of the afflicted birds but the results have been far from rewarding. In most cases they have succeeded in saving only a few hundred birds. The feathers of birds that come in contact with oil lose their compactness and water-shedding properties, the birds become chilled, lose the power of flight, are unable to hunt for food and the oil furthermore enters their digestive tracts. The result is obvious: slow but certain death. Oil spilled from tankers furthermore soils beaches and shores for a long time after.

ADVERSE EFFECTS OF THE PROTECTION
OF CERTAIN SEA BIRDS

On many islands where birds were strictly protected in wild-life reserves, certain species began to multiply rapidly and their numbers showed a marked increase. This was true parti-cularly of various species of gulls. Thus, for example, on the island of Walney off the west coast of England north of Li-verpool, there were only 120 pairs of herring gulls in 1947 and today some 17,000 pairs nest there. Another colony, on the Isle of May off Scotland's east coast, which started out with only several pairs of herring gulls in 1907, has over the decades grown to about 15,000 pairs. Until recently the her-ring gull was protected throughout the whole year also on the coasts of Germany and other European maritime countries. In West Germany and Denmark it has multiplied consider-ably. Its increased numbers however have made it impossible for other species of birds to nest where it occurs. The same thing happened in the islands of the North Sea. Here the herring gull had practically no natural enemies and was fur-thermore protected by man. However, after a time it began to pose a threat to the bird populations on the neighbouring islands, which were breeding grounds of terns, ducks and other birds, for it robbed their nests of eggs and newly hatched young as well. For this reason it is now permitted to kill this gull in West Germany and to collect its eggs. In recent years, however, the herring gull has also settled in the Baltic Sea off the coast of East Germany, where it previously nested only rarely. Today the coast teems with thousands of pairs of these gulls. They have also begun to multiply in large numbers on the coast of southern Sweden. As they cause great damage to the nests of ducks and other birds wherever they occur the conservationists are also considering regulating their number, mostly by collecting their eggs.

The great black-backed gull, which until recently was

a rare nester on Europe's shores, has also begun to multiply rapidly as a result of protective measures. In England and Wales it was on the point of extinction, with no more than 600 pairs nesting there in 1930. Today, however, the number has risen to more than 2,200 pairs. It has shown the same rapid increase on the eastern coast of the United States, where it nested for the first time in 1916. This large gull feeds mostly on the Manx shearwater, rabbits, young gulls, puffins as well as fish remnants. An over-population of seagulls on some offshore islands may entirely decimate the other small bird populations. Terns sometimes comprise as much as fifty per cent of the diet of sea gulls. In one colony of avocets, nesting on the English island of Havergate, a bird sanctuary belonging to the Royal Society for the Protection of Birds, black-headed gulls were once responsible for killing practically all the young.

In the Camargue, narcotics were added to the bait used to control the raptorial gulls and in some places in Holland, bait was poisoned with strychnine. Sterilization of adult birds is another of the methods that has been tried.

In recent years certain species of gulls are settling in cities, e.g. the kittiwake, whose droppings cause unsightly damage to buildings.

BIBLIOGRAPHY

Berrill, N. J. and M. : *The Life on Sea Islands.* New York — Toronto — London 1969.

Bruun, B. and Singer, A. : *The Hamlyn Guide to Birds of Britain and Europe.* London 1970.

Cramp, S., Bourne, W. R. P. and Saunders, S. : *The Seabirds of Britain and Ireland.* London 1974.

Fisher, J. and Lockley, R. M. : *Sea-Birds.* London 1954.

Heinzel, H., Fitter, R., Parslow, J. : *The Birds of Britain and Europe with North Africa and the Middle East.* London 1972.

Lockley, R. M. : *Ocean Wanderers: The Migratory Sea Birds of the World.* London — Vancouver 1974.

Robbins, C. S., Bruun, B., Zim, H. S. and Singer, A. : *Birds of North America: a Guide to Field Identification.* New York 1966.

Saunders, D. : *Seabirds.* London 1973.

Voous, K. : *Atlas of European Birds,* London 1960.

INDEX OF COMMON NAMES

INDEX OF LATIN NAMES